!

THE A-Z OF SERVICE EXCELLENCE

CATE SCHRECK

Testimonials

One of the biggest challenges facing business today is managing customer expectations. We live in a world that is moving from transactional interactions to meaningful engagement and Cate Schreck gets that. Her new book *The A-Z of Service Excellence* is an excellent guide to not just meeting expectations but exceeding them, regardless of the business you are in. A hugely valuable book, wonderfully thought out and written, and hugely practical.

Andrew Griffiths
Australia's #1 Small Business and Entrepreneurial Author

Cate is a forward thinking developer of skills and initiatives within the customer service arena and she imparts this knowledge with passionate enthusiasm. I have learnt much from Cate in relation to her determination to change the way we traditionally view the implementation of customer service skills and how she empowers employees to know their value in the workplace.

Maryanne Gardiner
Manager – Education Design

Cate is a one-of-a-kind customer service trainer. Her passion for giving individuals and teams the skills to provide consistently superior levels of customer service shows in both her preparation and delivery of service excellence training programs. If you want more customers, less customer complaints and happier staff then I highly recommend Cate.

Paul Steed – Managing Director
apd Australia

Cate designed and delivered a professional behaviours session for our team that was compelling, contemporary and highly relevant. Staff came to me with unsolicited positive feedback and I too was left feeling confident and motivated. Cate has a genuine passion for people working together in harmony in the workplace and her positive attitude is infectious.

Anita Roseblade – General Manager
Accounting Practice

Cate is a pleasure to work with as she listens to the needs of the business and adapts her style to suit accordingly. Cate has helped shift the mindset of how we manage and work with others and her knowledge and use of practical tools such as the DISC model, enabled individuals to gain greater levels of self-awareness and help them adapt their working and communication style to suit others.

Aine Murphy – HR Manager
MAB Corporation

Cate has provided over 25 fun and interactive workshops for our administrative and clinical staff across Australia. Cate goes to great lengths to understand a business and has the passion, skills and knowledge to deliver customer service skills training in a way that staff at all levels can relate to.

Craig Pritchard – National Field Development Manager
Back In Motion Health Group

Cate's positive approach and passion for training is contagious. Her professionalism and determination to deliver exceptional customer service is what makes Cate a dynamic and outstanding trainer, coach and mentor.

Lauren Baird
National HR Business Partner

Cate originally designed and delivered a 'first class customer service' training session for our Vic/Tas franchisees which was really well received. Since then, Cate has delivered further service skills training programs for our growing teams, including those in New Zealand. Cate has an engaging manner and delivers with enthusiasm and passion.

Ross Morley – Managing Director
GJ Gardner Homes Vic/Tas

It doesn't matter what industry you work in and your trailer load of qualifications count for little if you don't possess the skills of communication and engagement. Cate Schreck's training style and mode of delivery assist people to develop both and understand how to use them to the best of their abilities. Cate's visit to our school has allowed staff to better understand their own strengths and how to work better as a cohesive team. "Princess Fiona" as we now refer to Cate, will certainly be invited back because trainers and facilitators with high levels of emotional intelligence and a very full bag of ideas and strategies are very hard to find.

Brian Howley – Careers Manager
Victoria

Having interviewed Cate on my radio program about her training that aims to empower customer service providers, I can say you will not get a more passionate and committed advocate for the benefits of a healthy approach to helping individuals enjoy workplace interactions.

Dr Linda Wilson
Stress Management Specialist/Corporate Wellness Consultant

Cate has been vital in the rejuvenation of the Give Where You Live Foundation's 50th Loaned Executive Program. Cate's wonderful energy and professionalism has made working with her a breeze, and her ability to instil confidence in our participants has resulted in rave reviews from those involved. Cate's generosity and desire to help is outstanding and she has certainly gone above and beyond for our Foundation.

Jessica Young – Business Partnerships Manager
Give Where You Live Foundation

Cate's time with our opportunity shop volunteer teams was inspirational. Engaging our teams, who choose to be with Lifeline to support our life-saving work, can be quite a challenge especially when many volunteers have no previous retail experience. Cate's interactions were respectful and inquiring, building the trust and confidence that encouraged our volunteers to learn, actively participate and have fun.

Meredith Ericson – Chief Executive Officer
Lifefline South West Victoria

About the author

My first customer service job was in a local variety store in a small country town in Western Victoria, Australia. I was 15 years old and employed to work after school on Friday nights and again on Saturday mornings. My role initially was to tidy the store and show customers where products were, but eventually I graduated to the cash register and processing purchases. In my induction to the role, I was told to be bright and friendly and always ask if I didn't know the answer to customer questions. Customer service at this stage was easy: be nice, be polite and ask if you don't know what to do. This seemed like common sense to me – and so began my customer service journey.

The following provides a peek into my career so far and the steps I have taken that motivated me to start Lightbulb Training Solutions and become a Service Excellence Coach.

Climbing the ladder and finding new ladders

After working in the variety store, my next step was into full-time employment. For 18 months I worked as a pharmacy assistant, and then moved on to work in one of Australia's largest banks. The bank provided staff with many avenues for learning both sales and service skills, and over a career of more than 16 years with this employer, I progressed to become a customer service manager, commenced a diploma of business in frontline management and was regularly awarded and rewarded for my high level of service provision. During this time I also discovered my passion for educating and motivating people, and I was routinely appointed to design and deliver internal staff training sessions.

As time went on, however, the banking industry and I were no longer a good fit and I was ready for new challenges. I applied for and achieved a role as a disability employment consultant. My customers now were referred to as clients, and I was also working with their family members, the relevant support services and, of course, their employers. The role required me to gain training and assessment qualifications and I also chose to study a diploma of counselling.

When I applied for this job, I was competing against over 30 candidates, many of whom had previous experience in the disability industry. So why did they choose me? According to my new employer, it was my positive attitude, my clear desire to help others and my professional and confident demeanour. In other words, I had successfully transitioned from banking to disability employment on the strength of my soft skills – or, as I like to call them, my people skills.

I now felt unstoppable. I knew what my strengths were – soft skills – and I knew what I was passionate about – helping people achieve career success. I completed my diploma of business in frontline management and used my Workplace Trainer and Assessor qualification to become a contract trainer and assessor working for universities, registered training organisations and TAFEs. I was soon being contracted to train and assess business and retail qualifications for individuals and businesses of all sizes across Victoria.

Helping people up the ladder

In light of what I had learned so far in my career, and especially while I was providing training and assessment services to various businesses, one thing was clear: specialist customer service skills training available to businesses was lacking. Businesses ached for tailored and practical customer service skills training that educated and motivated their employees to be better than good. They wanted employees to be customer service professionals. Equally, employees ached for the skills that would help them deal with difficult customers, improve their job satisfaction and help them self-manage stress – and still have energy after work. They wanted to know how to become customer service professionals.

So in 2010, myself and my husband Steve, commenced Lightbulb Training Solutions (LTS). LTS is a specialist customer service training provider that uses a six-step ACTION method to help businesses across Australia create teams of customer service professionals. I love what I do so you, the customer service provider, can love what you do, too.

Author acknowledgements

Thank you to my friends and family who listened to me waffle about this book and also allowed me to say 'No' to getting together. 'I'm busy writing' must have sounded so lame but my husband, Steve, will confirm that I was completely unable to engage – on any level – when the book decided it needed attention.

To my husband, Steve: every day in every way you remind me it's okay to be me. You also make me laugh until my sides hurt and I know you would move mountains to keep me safe. I can't guarantee I won't write another book but I will – at least for now – stop getting up at 3 am to write and saying the words, 'Can't talk – writing'.

To my mum and dad, my brother, Anthony, and my sister, Sue. I'm sure Tim would find something amusing to say about what we have been up to and he would still ruin the family photo with his inability to keep a straight face and keep his hands down. Thank you for always encouraging me to try, always catching me when I fall and always seeing the positive in everything.

I have been totally surrounded by amazing entrepreneurs and people I call my 'book buddies' – Paul, Cathy and Mel, in particular. Many more of you have helped and I thank you all for answering my questions, keeping me on track and supplying me with your wisdom. Writing a book can be lonely but not with these people ready and willing to cheer you on.

As research for this book, I have had the great pleasure of interviewing some incredibly passionate customer service professionals from across Australia and New Zealand. You all not only gave me your time but also allowed me into your workplaces and proudly gave me your wisdom – and you should be proud. Customer service professionals work hard – often for little or no recognition. I recognise you and I, and all of your customers, thank you.

And then there is you: the person reading this book. Thank you for reading and thank you for wanting to make other people's days just a little bit better. I wish you nothing but success in your career and with your goal to become and remain a customer service professional. You cannot fail.

National Library of Australia Cataloguing-in-Publication entry:

Creator:	Schreck, Cate, author.
Title:	The A-Z of service excellence: the essential guide to becoming a customer service professional / Cate Schreck.
ISBN:	9780995357204 (paperback)
Subjects:	Customer services.
	Customer relations.
	Organizational behavior.
	Employees –Training of.
Dewey Number:	658.812

Project management and text design by Michael Hanrahan Publishing
Cover design by Peter Reardon

Contents

INTRODUCTION

Everyone you meet will no doubt have a 'horror' story about dealing with a business and their customer service representative. Since you are a customer service person yourself, you know every story has two sides, but in your heart you'd like to think you could have prevented such a horror story ever occurring. Indeed, you'd like to be considered, and regularly complimented for being, an excellent customer service person.

Regardless of the industry you work in, the products or services your business provides, or the age, gender, cultural background, hat or shoe size of your customers, your employer and all your customers want you to be confident, motivated and focused on providing excellent service to every customer, every day.

With over 30 years' experience in providing customer service across various industries, more than 20 years spent designing and delivering customer service training, and 15 years managing customer service teams, I know what it takes to become a highly valued and consistently complimented customer service person. I call such a person a 'customer service professional' – and it's exactly this person that this book is aimed at.

Defining a customer service professional

A customer service professional is a very special person – and someone who is highly valued in every workplace. Customer service professionals have the skills to interact with people so well that customers and employers alike rave about them for all the right reasons.

Customer service professionals have increased levels of job and personal satisfaction, and lower levels of stress. They know that nothing sells and nothing satisfies like excellent service, and they have a well-stocked 'toolbox' of customer service skills, knowledge and experiences so they are prepared to handle every customer service situation – including the good, the bad and the ugly.

To clarify further, here are the top 10 attributes of a customer service professional:

1. They have high-level people skills.
2. They can adapt their communication style to suit and delight every customer.
3. They willingly help other staff provide excellent service.
4. Their customers regularly compliment them on their service.
5. They handle customer complaints with ease.
6. They can be relied upon to represent a business professionally.
7. They are top sellers, because customers willingly buy what they offer.
8. They proactively keep their product and service knowledge up to date.
9. They seek to find solutions to service problems.
10. Their employers want to keep them and keep them happy.

This book is all about offering you insights into how you can become a customer service professional.

Defining a customer

Every business has two types of customers: internal and external. The following sections outline these two types.

Internal customers

These are the people who wear the uniform of the business. They include your co-workers and anyone who delivers a service on behalf of your employer. You provide service to your internal customers – usually referred to as the 'internal chain' of customer service. This chain captures the people carrying out tasks that ultimately produce the product or service for an external customer.

External customers

These are the people who choose to do business with you – and are the customers this book is designed to delight. Of course, the term 'customer' is not used in every workplace. You might find your 'customers' are referred to by one of the following terms:

- attendee
- buyer
- client
- consumer
- guest/visitor
- parent/guardian
- patient
- patron
- prospect/lead
- purchaser
- shopper
- student.

Regardless of the term that is used in your industry, however, the meaning is the same: they are people who need your help to access the products or services your business provides.

For continuity and to minimise confusion, I use the term 'customer' throughout this book when referring to all these types of people.

Who this book is suited to

Whether you are seeking your first customer service role, a new customer service role or have been providing customer service for many years, this book is for you. Indeed, many jobs include aspects of customer service, even if they are not clearly stated in the position title or role description.

Roles that require customer service skills include the following:

- accountant/financial planner
- administrator/receptionist
- advisor/evaluator/salesperson
- help desk operator/support person
- agent/consultant
- aid/carer/support worker/nurse
- beauty therapist/hairdresser/nail technician
- call centre operator
- clerk/teller
- coach/personal trainer
- concierge/maître d'/host
- developer/manager
- officer/representative
- shop or store assistant
- waiter/waitress/wait staff.

If your job title is included in the preceding list, this book is for you. Even if your job title is not included, still consider if you are required to interact with customers. If you do, this book is also for you.

If you have been providing customer service for many years, or even decades, in the same business or across several businesses, you may think you have nothing more to learn. Maybe you have even started to find customer interactions quite demanding, or the idea of a job without customers has become rather appealing. Perhaps you are simply tired of dealing with people.

If you relate to or agree with these sentiments, congratulations for being honest. I too reached a point in my career where the idea of a job with no customer interactions was so appealing that I spent time searching for that job. (If you're inclined to do the same, I'll save you some time here – no job is without interactions with people.)

My customer service journey brought up some serious questions:

- What happened that made me want to consider a job with no people interaction?
- Why, when I am generally a friendly and happy person, did customer service become hard work?
- What changed so that I now find interactions with people the most rewarding and satisfying part of my work day?

All of these questions and more are answered in this book – along with how you can take a similar journey.

> **If you've lost your passion for providing excellent service, please read on. I was you once and I wrote this book to help you.**

How to get the most out of this book

This book contains everything you need to know about customer service – it is an 'A to Z', after all. So think of this book just like other reference books (although hopefully not as dry as some reference books can be). You can read the book cover to cover or you can dip into certain areas, based on what you need help with right now. You can also take this book with you on your career journey, rereading certain topics as needed, because the information and skills contained within these pages suit all industries and all levels of customer service. Even if you move out of a predominantly customer service role, you will still be dealing with people and that's what this book is full of – help with building skills to deal with people.

Every chapter begins with some wise words and I've also included what I like to refer to as 'light bulb moments' throughout chapters. These are summaries or specific tips or strategies, and are highlighted by a light bulb icon (just like the one a little earlier). I find these quotes and light bulb moments inspiring, and I refer back to them when I need to be reminded that the skills I have are valuable – and that to keep them sharp I too must take the time to refresh them. I hope they provide the same help to you.

So now it's time to jump in. Pick a topic that you need help with or simply start at the beginning and launch into attitude.

A

IS FOR ATTITUDE

*A bad attitude is like a flat tyre;
you're not going anywhere until
you change it.*

ANONYMOUS

When was the last time you received amazing customer service? I mean, really amazing. When you were so impressed that you told friends and family, and knew you would happily go back to that business again and again. What was it about the service that was so amazing?

And when was the last time you had a terrible customer service experience? I mean the type that left you so frustrated or angry that you told your friends and family all about it, and vowed to never return to that business. What was it about that experience that was so bad?

Most of the things we assess as excellent customer service are related to the attitude of the customer service provider. Similarly, most of the things we assess as terrible service also relate to the attitude of the service provider.

> The good news: your customer service attitude is 100 per cent within your control.

The power of a positive attitude

I grew up in a small country town in Western Victoria and when I went shopping, customer service was almost always provided by someone I knew. So the experience was very much like having a conversation with a friend. Friendly greetings were exchanged, along with pleasantries about family and perhaps a quick discussion about a current event in the town, and then you gave the other person payment for what you wanted to purchase.

When I started shopping outside of my small country town, strangers provided the customer service and that made the interaction a little different. Some strangers were nice and straightaway treated me like a friend, and so the interaction was positive. Others barely looked at me, didn't want to talk to me or were insincere in the way they greeted me. Their service provision made me feel like I was an interruption to their day. Sound familiar?

Can you remember the first time you were a customer and what the experience was like? If you were like me, your first experience as a customer was when buying lollies. I was the kid that stood at the glass cabinet and asked for, '1 of those, and 2 of those and, no, maybe 3 of those and – how much is that and how much do I have left?' Mixed lollies may indeed be the reason there were so many grumpy customer service providers in the 1970s and '80s. How we were treated in our formative years as a customer may have had an impact on our current expectations of customer service providers, and our perception of whether or not it has a valuable role in society. And everyone tends to remember the negative experiences over the positive ones.

Choosing the right customer service attitude is exactly that – a choice. Every day we make choices. From the moment we wake up we choose what to wear, what to eat, who to associate with and what to buy. Some choices we make without really considering the consequences of the decision. And sometimes that's okay. Choosing to come to work with a negative attitude, however, can definitely have negative consequences. Customer service professionals make a conscious effort to choose a positive attitude every day, because they know how powerful the right attitude can be – not only for them, but also for everyone they interact with.

When you make the choice to be positive, you can look forward to five things:

1. fewer complaints – customers prefer to do business with happy people
2. more sales and/or better business outcomes – customers trust people who can focus
3. reduced stress – customers never complain about genuine smiles
4. increased productivity – co-workers prefer to work with positive people
5. job security – employers want positive and productive staff.

Proving you have a great customer service attitude

Customer service excellence is as much about projecting a positive attitude as it is about your actions. The more positive your attitude towards your role as a service provider, the more positive the attitude you project to your customers. But remember: saying you have a positive attitude is great, but actions speak louder than words.

Here are some examples of a great customer service attitude:

- apologising for a delay or a mistake
- being punctual
- ceasing conversations with a co-worker when a customer needs your help
- ceasing unrelated activities when interacting with a customer
- giving eye contact to a person who is talking to you
- listening without interrupting
- offering a seat for the frail or elderly
- opening the door for people
- refraining from eating or drinking in the view of customers or when talking on the phone
- remembering and acknowledging customer events (for example, birthdays and celebrations)
- saying please when you ask for something
- seeking and using your customer's name
- smiling when you greet people
- thanking customers for waiting
- wearing neat and clean clothes or uniform.

It's important to remember that not all workplaces will deem everything on the preceding list as necessary or, in some cases, possible. To prove to your employer that you have a positive customer service attitude, ask which items on the list they believe are possible and best suited to the customers of the business. Your employer may also have other ideas to add to the list.

Staying positive when you feel negative

Rude or angry customers, unexpected changes, delays or errors can all have a negative effect on even the most positive customer service providers. This means on some days you will be required to make a greater effort to remain positive, and those are the times when choosing the right attitude will serve you very well. Customer service professionals find when they make a conscious effort to change their own negative attitude, the feedback and thanks they get from customers and co-workers is well worth the effort.

When we choose to remain calm and professional in the tough times, we can effectively help change the mood of those around us as well. Customer service professionals have the skills to handle difficult people, balance the day-to-day demands of their role and still keep themselves and those around them calm. To help them with this, customer service professionals have one unbeatable weapon: a positive attitude.

At times, situations in our personal lives and/or our mental and physical health can have a negative impact on our emotions. There have certainly been times in my career when, no matter how hard I tried, leaving those difficult thoughts and feelings at home was quite a challenge – and not one that I always succeeded in. When those times happen, be clear that your employer would prefer you to disclose your situation. Employers have a responsibility to provide every employee with a safe workplace. One employee who is not able to complete their role safely or finds it difficult to interact with co-workers professionally can make it difficult for those around them to also remain productive and, in some cases, safe. You also have a duty of care to those you work with, so let your employer know what's going on so they can consider the best steps for the workplace as a whole.

> Acknowledging when you need help is a sign of a customer service professional.

Customer service professionals know that when they're not feeling their best, their mood may have a negative impact on everyone they interact with. They also know that faking a positive attitude is hard work, and so sustainable only for a short time. Customers today can pick a 'faker' from a mile away and your co-workers, who know you so well, will easily be able to identify when you're not at your usual positive and service-focused best.

So be kind to yourself and be honest with your employer, and take the time and support you need to recharge your customer service batteries.

Attitude action

Before you start your workday, take a moment to con-sider how you feel and what attitude you are bringing into the workplace. Customers and co-workers prefer to interact with people who have a positive attitude. If something negative is on your mind, acknowledge it, write it down if you have to and make a deal with yourself that you will pay it the attention it needs – after work.

Remember that a positive attitude is contagious – go and infect someone today.

B

IS FOR BEHAVIOURAL STYLES

*Customers are sometimes like family.
We don't always get to choose them
and it's inevitable that with some of
them we will clash.*

ANONYMOUS

When starting to think about your customer service behavioural style, ask yourself the following questions:

- Do you find some customers easy to communicate with and others more challenging?
- Do you find yourself sometimes puzzled or annoyed by customers' expectations?

- Do you wonder why some customers make quick decisions and others take forever?
- Do you wish all customers were easy to interact with?

We all face situations when our typical approach or communication, which often works so well, just does not achieve the results we expected. How we behave makes perfect sense to us, but sometimes others do not respond how we thought they would and, in some cases, seem to be annoyed or take offence at our approach. People very rarely set out to cause upset – they just behave differently because they are different. If you've experienced a reaction you weren't expecting from a customer, no doubt you then tried a different approach, but this process is often hit or miss, and so can be frustrating and unproductive.

I've felt like this many times throughout my career, with both co-workers and customers. I worked hard to build strong workplace relationships but I still found myself avoiding working with certain people and dreading serving some customers.

When I left the bank I engaged the services of a career coach and she introduced me to personality and behavioural style assessments. What I learned from these about myself and the styles of others, and how to use this knowledge to communicate with others, created a series of true 'light bulb moments'. With this knowledge and further training, I have been able to adjust my behaviour to become a more confident and effective communicator, negotiator, motivator and educator. I found this information so life changing that I studied further and am now an Accredited Consultant and Facilitator of DISC ADVANCED® behavioural style assessments.

The DISC behavioural style model

Behavioural and personality models are widely used around the world, especially in psychometrics and psychometric testing (personality assessments and tests). These models have also been used by philosophers, leaders and managers as an aid to understanding, explaining and managing communications and relationships. Used appropriately, psychometrics and personality tests can be hugely beneficial in improving knowledge of self and other people.

In other words, the more you understand about personality and behavioural styles, the more you start to realise how others may perceive you and react to you, and vice versa.

Within these models, DISC is a very popular behavioural style model attributed to the work of several researchers and theorists, one of whom was Dr William Moulton Marston. Marston had many accomplishments to his name – not only was he a lawyer and psychologist but he also helped produced the first functional lie detector (or polygraph), authored self-help books and created the *Wonder Woman* character and comic. His major contribution to psychology came when he generated the DISC characteristics of emotions and behaviours of normal people. He published his findings in *Emotions of Normal People*, published in 1928.

Dr Marston explained that people illustrate their emotions using four behaviour types, covered in the following section.

Identifying the four DISC styles

The first of the DISC styles is the D Style, which stands for Dominance or Driver, and is used for people who are fast-paced and task-focused. To identify someone within the D Style, look for someone who:

- often appears to be in a hurry
- is direct, says what they think
- interrupts
- becomes irritated easily
- wants to know 'What's the bottom line?'

The I Style stands for Influencing or Inspiring and highlights people who are fast-paced and people-focused. Someone who is I Style:

- is open and friendly
- talks a lot
- is animated
- does not listen for long
- may ask the same question several times.

The S Style stands for Stable or Supportive and can be used for people who are slower paced and people-focused. Someone who is S Style:

- listens carefully
- is easy going
- appears thoughtful
- does not get easily excited
- finds completely new ideas can make them uncomfortable.

Finally, the C Style stands for Concise or Correctness and groups people who are slower paced and task-focused. A C Style person:

- appears reserved and somewhat timid
- focuses on details
- studies specifications carefully
- may do homework or research before making a decision
- proceeds cautiously.

As you can see, each style has a preferred pace and focus. Have a think about the descriptions for each style, and consider which style you more strongly lean towards.

DISC in the workplace

Dr Marston's work, combined with many other experts, was developed into a DISC assessment questionnaire that has been used by more than 50 million people since it was first introduced in 1972. Organisations today ask potential and existing employees to complete DISC assessments for various reasons, including to:

- understand the strengths and possible development areas of job applicants
- predict co-worker communication challenges
- create motivational workplace environments
- re-deploy staff to more suitable roles
- create balanced and supportive teams
- identify development opportunities for individuals
- identify areas of potential employee stress
- develop action plans to meet the career goals of employees.

As a DISC ADVANCED® Accredited Consultant and Facilitator, I use the DISC theory to help customer service providers understand their own behavioural style and to identify the style of those they interact with. I then provide the training they need so they can adapt their behaviour to develop strong and trusting relationships with their customers and co-workers.

When using DISC theory, remembering the following is important:

- No one style is better than the others – each style has strengths.
- All of us have the ability to use all four styles.
- You will likely identify with more than one style.
- DISC assessments identify which of the four styles you find most natural and, in turn, take less of your energy.

DISC case study

When you have an understanding of DISC theory and you know your natural style, you can then more accurately predict how the tasks of a job and the workplace environment may affect your chances of long-term success in the role.

To understand this more fully, let's look at an example – in this case, how each style may react to being in a call centre operator role. Firstly, here are the characteristics of the role:

- *Job title:* full-time call centre operator.
- *Workplace environment:* sharing an open-plan office with over 30 staff.
- *Duties:* respond to inbound customer complaint telephone calls, attend twice weekly staff meetings and use company database to record customer complaint and resolution details.
- *Targets:* aim to finalise calls within five minutes, ensure average caller waiting times are no more than eight minutes and aim for 70 per cent of calls to be resolved in the first instance.
- *Wage:* standard call centre rate, with bonus payments for individuals who exceed targets.

The following sections outline how people within each of the four DISC styles might react to working in this role. Note that these examples use a person who has a strong identification with one style only and that, in reality, most people identify with more than one style.

D Style

A person within this style is motivated by the chance to win. They would be energised by the targets and enjoy the open office environment because it would allow them to monitor their competition. Meetings that include public recognition for achieving targets would also be appealing. D Styles are task focused and rarely take things personally, so they would have little or no problem dealing with difficult callers.

This means the majority of this role would suit the D Style person, but to do the role successfully and over a long period of time, they may need to make a conscious effort to be considerate of the customer's feelings, to listen without interrupting and to offer verbal empathy to help the customer feel respected and not rushed.

I Style

An I Style person likes to interact with people and they will enjoy the open office environment and not be bothered by the noise of co-workers. They are naturally positive people who care about others, and are motivated by helping others and solving problems. The I Style feels uncomfortable being disliked or not being able to help, so customers or co-workers who are annoyed with them, or suggest they are unhelpful, can dent the I Style confidence.

The majority of this role would suit the I Style person, but to do it successfully and over a long period of time, they may need to be able to de-brief their concerns and have access to support after difficult interactions.

S Style

A person within the S Style also likes to help people but they may be more productive in a calmer workplace with less noise and fewer chances of being interrupted. They like to take the time to ask questions and believe that listening builds trust and gives them a greater insight into the needs of an individual. The time limits that form part of the role requirements would suggest they would have to rush upset customers. They may also be conflicted by not being able to provide a more comprehensive service – for example, conduct a follow-up call to confirm the customer is fully satisfied.

The S Style may not find individual competition rewarding and may be more motivated by shared team goals, which means a large part of this role would require an S Style to work outside of their comfort zone. This doesn't mean an S Style could not do the role, but to do it successfully and over a long period of time, they would need to use more energy.

C Style

The C Style person would rather work alone or at least away from noise and interruptions. They dislike conflict and prefer to do research before making decisions. They seek to do things correctly and believe that doing tasks quickly and with little or no attention to detail is a recipe for disaster. Interaction with co-workers is not high on their list of priorities so unless the team meeting has defined actions and clear outcomes, they may not participate with enthusiasm.

These attributes mean this role would require a C Style to work predominantly outside of their comfort zone. This doesn't mean they could not do the role, but to do it successfully and over a long period of time, they would need to use more energy.

> When you know your natural behavioural style, why some work tasks require more energy and how the work environment can impact on your job satisfaction become clear.

Adapting your style for success

Think of the people in your life who you communicate with easily. You will probably find that they share a similar behavioural style to you. We will naturally find communicating with people with a style that is familiar to us requires less energy. Alternatively, styles that are different to ours may require us to work a little harder to build a stronger relationship.

Customer service professionals aim to communicate in a way that makes it easier for the customer to understand and do business with them – and a 'one size fits all' approach to providing excellent customer service doesn't exist. When we consider the behavioural style of a customer and then adjust our communication to suit their style, we go a long way to building a sense of trust. A customer will respect your approach (because, after all, it's like theirs).

In psychometrics, the act of adapting your style to someone else's is referred to as 'stretching'. The amount of stretch required for you to adapt your style to suit your customers depends on how different their style is to yours. And, as with any stretching, it's much easier to stretch your style when you 'warm up' – in other words, you benefit greatly from practising using those behaviours that are least natural to you. Knowing how to communicate with a different style has other benefits too – you can not only adapt your way of communicating but also allow yourself a chance to restore your energy after the interaction.

> Excellent customer service is *not* treating customers how *you* want to be treated; excellent customer service *is* treating customers how *they* want to be treated.

I have shared with you here only a small amount of DISC knowledge. As a DISC ADVANCED® Accredited Consultant and Facilitator, it is my responsibility to not only pass on the information but also make sure that those with the knowledge understand it fully and use it wisely.

With this in mind, noting the following is important:

- Use the DISC information in this chapter as a guide only and remember that all four styles have positive strengths.
- Different styles from yours do not equal wrong. Rather, different styles equal different strengths.
- If you want to know your dominant style, you can access online behavioural and personality profile assessments. Some will be quite simple and others more thorough. For best results and to obtain value for money, any psychometric assessments are best conducted by a qualified assessor who can also explain the model and provide you with a full interpretation of your results. Psychometric assessments conducted without support can leave you with more questions than answers.

Behavioural styles action

You will always find it easier to interact with someone of the same behavioural style as you, but you can also start to master interacting with people of different styles. Next time you interact with a customer who displays a different style from you, consider adapting how you communicate to suit them. These simple adjustments can make a big difference in how a customer perceives you.

For a D style person:

- be direct and specific
- do not dominate
- act quickly – they decide fast
- enjoy the battle
- do not be emotional.

With someone who is I Style:

- be bright and friendly – do not ignore
- schedule time for chatting
- let them speak
- speak about people and feelings
- have fun.

With an S Style person:

- focus on people
- present issues logically
- be sincere – do not dominate
- provide the information they need
- slow down and allow time for questions.

For a C Style person:

- provide facts
- be patient – slow down
- give plenty of detailed information
- do not pressure them for an answer or decision
- do not talk about personal issues.

C

IS FOR COMMUNICATION

A smile costs nothing,
and the returns are high.

RICHARD BRANSON

We develop our communication skills from a very early age and, unless we have undertaken formal communication training – which most of the population haven't – we may have picked up some bad communication habits without even knowing it. In our formative years, we often mimic those around us and so we develop our communication style simply through watching and listening to others.

Good communication skills can help you to avoid conflict, gain respect and solve problems. Open and honest communication is important for establishing a good relationship with your customers, which will inevitably help you to gain their trust and provide them with a level of service that exceeds their expectations.

Communication is a key skill that customer service providers need to master to become customer service professionals. Every time we communicate with our customers, we need to focus on not only what we are saying, but also how we are saying it.

Of course, literally thousands of books and resources are available to you that are dedicated to the art of being an effective communicator. Rather than trying to condense all of that information into one chapter, I have decided to focus on the two areas of communication you are most likely to use in your role as a customer service provider: face-to-face and telephone.

Face-to-face communication

Face-to-face communication means exactly that: you are in the same physical location as your customer. It doesn't include communication via Skype or other visual programs because they limit your ability to give and gain 100 per cent of the message. In a true face-to-face situation, a lot more communicating is going on than just the words that are spoken. Even when silent, we are always sending signals to others in a face-to-face situation, whether we like it or not.

In a face-to-face situation we communicate how we feel and what our attitude is in three ways: body language, tone of voice and actual words. Of these, according to research by Albert Mehrabian published in his 1971 book *Silent Messages*, a perhaps surprising 55 per cent comes from our body language, while 38 per cent comes from tone of voice. This means a tiny 7 per cent of how we feel and what our attitude is comes from the actual words we use.

Body language

Much debate exists about body language and how to interpret it. The following table highlights what certain body language signals commonly mean in Western society. Although this table is a guide only, customer service professionals can use it to form a more complete picture of what the customer may be feeling. Also remember that an individual's body language may be representative of other issues such as pain – both emotional and physical.

Body language	Interpretation
Facial expressions	
Frown	Displeasure, unhappiness
Smile	Friendliness, happiness
Narrowed eyes	Anger, confusion
Eye contact	
Glancing	Lack of interest
Steady	Active listening, interested
Staring	Rude, overbearing
Hand/arm gestures	
Pointing finger	Authority, displeasure, lecturing
Folded arms	Not open to change, stubborn
Arms at side	Open to suggestions, relaxed
Body postures	
Fidgeting	Bored, distracted
Hands on hips	Anger, defensive
Slouching in chair	Lack of interest
Clothing	
Neat business attire	Professional, reliable, responsible
Creased, unclean or ill-fitting attire	Disrespect, unreliable, careless

When communicating with customers and considering body language (yours and theirs), also be mindful of customers' personal space. People have personal space comfort zones for many reasons, based on culture, age and gender. Invading a person's space by standing too close or touching them can be viewed as disrespectful and can cause anxiety.

> Remember: actions speak louder than words.

Tone of voice

Your tone of voice when communicating is related to your volume, pitch and tempo. That is, your volume can be loud or soft, your pitch can be high or low and your tempo can be fast or slow. Each of these elements, and the way they can be combined in different ways, can create a very different impression from the words you use.

To further confirm how much your tone conveys information, consider how by simply emphasising a different word within a sentence, we can give people a completely different message. For example, say the following sentence out loud, placing more emphasis on the word in bold to see how this changes the interpretation:

- **I** didn't say she lost my keys. (Who said it then? Someone said it.)
- I **didn't** say she lost my keys. (I definitely didn't say it.)
- I didn't **say** she lost my keys. (But I implied it.)
- I didn't say **she** lost my keys. (So she didn't lose them, but someone did.)
- I didn't say she **lost** my keys. (But she did something with them.)
- I didn't say she lost **my** keys. (So it wasn't your keys?)
- I didn't say she lost my **keys**. (She lost something else then?)

Just as we can use our tone to let people know we are excited, unhappy, annoyed or tired, we can use our tone to advise our customers we are professional, reliable and focused on them.

> **Remember: it's not what you say but how you say it.**

Words

If only 7 per cent of the message about how we feel and what our attitude is comes from our actual words (as mentioned earlier in this chapter), then should we just shut up? No. What you say is, of course, of vital importance when you are communicating. You do need to be aware that, if your body language and tone of voice are sending negative or distracting messages, the chances of the person you are communicating with understanding or even listening to what you have to say is very limited. But once you're using body language and tone of voice more effectively, it's time to really harness the power of your words. The following sections show you how.

Avoid jargon

Jargon includes acronyms or terms used only in your workplace – for example, CSP (customer service professional) or Form B23. It can be easy to forget that customers don't necessarily understand the jargon and terms that you use every day. Not only can jargon be confusing but also some customers won't ask what a term or phrase means for fear of coming across as uneducated – they'll just walk away, dissatisfied with you and your company. Instead, use words that everyone can understand

– imagine you're talking to a friend or family member and use the kinds of words you would with them.

Mind your language

Your personal conduct speaks volumes about how you view your role. Using offensive language runs the risk of offending others and diminishing your credibility. While swearing or cursing on the outside of work hours may be common for some, offensive language of any kind is not recommend in any workplace.

> Your words convey information. Your body language and tone of voice confirm you are worth listening to.

Telephone communication

Have you ever called a business and, just by the way the person answered the phone, been able to determine if you wanted to talk to them and could trust them? Perhaps you also had an idea of what type of mood they were in or had even decided what they might look like? We often determine if we are going to like interacting with a person over the phone primarily by the tone of voice they use – not the words that they say. Indeed, again according to research by Albert Mehrabian published in his 1971 book *Silent Messages*, over the telephone, your tone of voice carries 85 per cent of the information about how you feel and what you attitude is, leaving your actual words to convey only 15 per cent.

One of the first things you need to master to be an effective telephone communicator is breathing control. Good breath control is a result of proper posture and good care of your physical health, particularly the lungs and diaphragm. You are not breathing effectively if you are slumped and slouching at your desk. Make it a habit to sit up straight when you talk on the telephone. You will also notice that the more physically fit you are, the better control you have over your lung capacity and the more effectively you speak.

If you are angry or upset, surprised or focused, callers will hear it in your voice; this is a quality people pay attention to. Although you cannot eliminate negative aspects of tone completely, you can manage them with concentration and practise.

Articulation, which is the way that your pronounce sound by using your mouth, lips and jaw to form words, is highly responsive to practise, so if you wish to change the way you pronounce things, practise can certainly make perfect.

The following sections provide some more tips for perfecting your telephone communication.

The four Es of an effective voice

To really use your tone of voice effectively with customers, use the four Es: be expressive, enunciate clearly, engage with customers and energise your voice.

Expressive

Use your voice to vary the tone, pitch and rate of what you say to make it interesting to hear – and make it clear you're interested in your customers.

Enunciate

Use clear enunciation and master articulation. We can be casual when speaking with friends or family – dropping a final consonant, like the 'g' in a word with an 'ing' ending, for example, or truncating the middle letters of a word. Unfortunately, when we do that on the telephone, the sound of these shortcuts gets exaggerated. Open your mouth and speak clearly.

Engage

Your voice should be smooth and pleasant, not whining or complaining. Communicate that you are happy in your work (and a happy person overall) in order to engage your caller. Speaking in anger or being curt will put your call – and your company – in a negative light.

Energise

Your voice needs to really shine when you use the telephone as your instrument. You need to feel energy and pass that positive flow through to your callers. This means that you approach your job as if it is the only thing that matters right now, and that the caller you currently have on the line is the most important caller ever.

Although it sounds corny and will probably feel uncomfortable sometimes, think about people you enjoy speaking to in your own life, and what it was that led you to talk to them or buy from them, or that made the conversation pleasant. Inject energy and joy into your voice and work from the attitude that you are there to serve your customer, and you will be more likely to meet your objective, whatever it is.

The 'three ring' process

Answering the phone promptly certainly gives the customer an impression of efficiency but if we rush to answer a phone and forget to focus on our tone of voice, we can give a customer the feeling that we are exactly that – rushed.

> We often speak faster and louder when we are in a hurry. Talking fast and loud on the phone is poor communication.

With this in mind, I created the 'three ring' process. As you will see, the focus of this process is on what you can do to sound professional, confident and ready to help your telephone customers. It's all about your tone.

Customer service professionals use the three ring process as follows:

1. *First ring:* Stop what you are doing and focus on how you are feeling. If you are busy, stressed or in any way less than positive and focused on answering the phone with a bright and friendly tone, take a deep breath and smile. A fake smile can take as little as six seconds to feel real and your body will respond with a little rush of those positive endorphins.

2. *Second ring:* Get a pen and paper ready to take notes. If you prefer to use the computer to take notes, be aware that your caller will hear you tapping away and this can be distracting and noisy. Confirm you are typing up notes so you get their details, information or needs correct.

3. *Third ring:* Answer the call and remember to keep that smile on your dial. When we smile, the corners of our mouth lift and so does the tone of our voice. Your workplace may wish for you to use a set greeting but as long as you say the business name and your name, you've started a customer interaction on the right foot.

Communication action

Record yourself during a telephone conversation and play it back. It doesn't have to be customer conversation, any conversation will do – just check first that the person on the other end is okay with you recording your chat. If you prefer, ask a trusted co-worker to play the role of a customer and run through a general conversation you would have with a customer. Avoid using a script because it is more difficult to sound genuine if you are reading set words.

Don't worry; most people dislike the sound of their own voice. The more you do this the more comfortable you will become with how you sound to others. When I first completed this activity (and moved past cringing at the sound of my own voice) I realised I had a habit of saying 'excellent' and 'actually' … a lot. I also was lazy with pronouncing the word 'thirty' – it sounded like 'thirdy'.

When you listen to yourself on the recording, your ears will very quickly pick up on how you can improve your telephone communication.

To help you with this process, when you listen to the recording, ask yourself these five questions:

- Do I sound genuinely interested in what the other person is saying?
- Do I interrupt?
- Do I use jargon?
- Do I speak clearly?
- Do I enunciate my words correctly?

D

IS FOR DETECTIVE

*Get closer than ever to your customers.
So close that you tell them what they need
well before they realise it themselves.*

STEVE JOBS

Customers of all businesses ache for their service providers to show great interest in them. They want to be listened to, they want to know the service provider understands them and their needs, and they are delighted if service providers treat those needs with a sense of urgency.

Customer service professionals think like detectives. As soon as they engage with a customer they are looking at their body language, listening to their tone of voice and their words, and asking questions so they can provide a level of customer service that leaves a customer feeling valued and respected.

How to think like a detective

I want you to start thinking like a detective and consider each of your individual customers as a unique and sometimes complicated puzzle. When you start to think of your customers as puzzles, you will find yourself becoming very interested in everything your customers say and do. And you will have solved the puzzle when you are crystal clear on your customers' expectations.

Thinking like a detective will also help you to avoid distractions, and allow you to give 100 per cent of your attention to your customer. Customers who feel they have 100 per cent of the attention of a customer service provider are more likely to buy from them, listen to them and thank them for their excellent service.

A word of warning, though: your aim is only to detect enough about your customer to provide excellent service. Be careful that you don't ask so many questions that your customer feels like you are interrogating them.

> Good detectives go about their work calmly and professionally, and often surprise customers with how much they have learned, with little or no intrusion.

The three Vs that make you a great detective

Customer service professionals seek to understand how a customer is feeling by assessing the 'three Vs' – that is, verbal, visual and vocal clues. When we use the three Vs to identify how customers feel, we can adjust our service to not only show we understand and care about them but also leave them feeling valued and respected.

Here's a breakdown of the three Vs and what they encompass:

- *verbal*: what the customer says
- *visual*: what the customer does
- *vocal*: how the customer sounds.

Understanding the three Vs with a case study

I recently went to the cinema and I think it would be fair to say that the customer (a mum) in front of me in the ticket line was not happy and excited to be there. She had her little girl with her, who was on a mission to empty the contents of Mum's bag onto the floor.

Here's how the interaction unfolded when the mum approached the ticket box:

- Customer service provider:
    - *Verbal*: 'What movie and how many tickets?'
    - *Visual*: Looking at the keyboard and typing.
    - *Vocal*: Monotone.

- Customer:
    - *Verbal*: 'Um, *Frozen* please – 1 adult and 1 child.'
    - *Visual*: Juggling child on hip and fumbling to put contents back into her bag.
    - *Vocal*: Frustrated and exhausted.

- Customer service provider:
    - *Verbal*: 'That will be $x.'
    - *Visual*: Still looking at the keyboard and typing.
    - *Vocal*: Monotone.

- Customer:
  - *Verbal:* 'Oh, okay. My daughter has emptied out my bag and I'm trying to find my purse.'
  - *Visual:* Searching desperately for her purse while balancing the child on her hip.
  - *Vocal:* Apologetic.

- Customer service provider:
  - *Verbal:* None.
  - *Visual:* Taking the money, passing over the tickets.
  - *Vocal:* None.

Now let's look at the same situation handled by a customer service professional:

- Customer service professional:
  - *Verbal:* 'Hi, looks like you've got your hands full. What movie would you like to see today?'
  - *Visual:* Smile and eye contact with both the lady and her child.
  - *Vocal:* Bright, genuine and friendly.

- Customer:
  - *Verbal:* 'I sure have. We would like to see *Frozen* please – 1 adult and 1 child.'
  - *Visual:* Juggling child on hip and fumbling to put contents back into her bag.
  - *Vocal:* Frustrated and exhausted.

- Customer service professional:
  - *Verbal:* 'Oh, she is going to love this film and you're going to love our comfy seats. That will be $x.'

- *Visual:* Smiling while printing up the tickets.
- *Vocal:* Bright, genuine and friendly.

• Customer:
  - *Verbal:* 'Oh, okay, I'll just find my purse as my daughter has emptied out my bag.'
  - *Visual:* Searching for her purse while balancing the child on her hip.
  - *Vocal:* Apologetic.

• Customer service professional:
  - *Verbal:* 'That's okay; you are doing a great job. Did you know you can book your tickets online? That will save you time and you won't have to line up. Here's a brochure that explains it all.'
  - *Visual:* Smiling and hands over the brochure.
  - *Vocal:* Bright, genuine and friendly.

• Customer:
  - *Verbal:* 'Thank you so much! I forgot I could do that.'
  - *Visual:* Shoulders relax, big smile emerges.
  - *Vocal:* Relief and genuine thanks.

This second version of the same situation confirms that it takes no more time to provide excellent service; it simply takes the right attitude and focus. Customer service professionals know that every customer interaction is an opportunity to exceed expectations – and that customers who are made to feel important and valued remember that feeling long after the interaction.

The TLC process

TLC is a popular acronym usually used for 'tender loving care', which is exactly how you want to be treating your customers. But TLC for customer service professionals stands for Think, Learn and Consider. This TLC process helps you gain a clearer and much deeper understanding of your individual customer's diverse needs and expectations.

T – Think like a customer

When trying to think like your customer would, ask yourself:

1. What three things do you think most of your customers would consider excellent service?
2. Do you do those three things?
3. How can you include those three things in your service provision?

L – Learn about your customers

Identify the segments your customers may fall into, learn about those segments and consider how you could incorporate that knowledge into your service provision.

For example, your customers could be divided into segments via the following:

- age
- culture
- physical health
- mental health
- education
- income
- gender
- language.

Of course, each customer will cross over the various segments. When you consider the diversity of your customer base and take the time to learn more about your customers' differences, you will find it easier to empathise with them and show respect.

C – Consider your customers' feelings

How do the products and services your business provides impact on the feelings of your customers? How a customer feels before they engage with you will impact on how they communicate with you, right from the start, and how you should communicate with them.

For example:

- Customers attending an entertainment business may be happy and excited.
- Customers seeing a medical practitioner may be unhappy, anxious or in pain.
- Customers buying a car could be excited, curious or guarded.

Detective action

When you take the time to consider how your customers might be feeling about engaging with you and your business, you can then adapt your own behaviour to be mindful of their feelings.

Complete the TLC process to give you a greater understanding of how your customers are thinking and feeling.

E

IS FOR EMOTIONAL INTELLIGENCE

Anyone can become angry – that is
easy … but to do this to the right person,
to the right extent, at the right time, with
the right motive, and in the right way, that
is not for everyone, nor is it easy.

ARISTOTLE

Much has been written about emotional intelligence – and more specifically its value in the workplace – but the concept of emotional intelligence is not new.

The preceding quote from Aristotle confirms that controlling our anger emotion is not easy. Indeed, years of research and testing has shown that the reason for this is that our human brains are hardwired to give emotions the upper hand. The limbic system (the emotional brain) reacts to events first, before we have the opportunity to engage the rational brain (cortex). This means our brain can quickly generate our 'fight or flight' response – but letting our limbic system take over may not always be the best reaction.

The five components of emotional intelligence

Emotional intelligence is not just about your emotional awareness and your ability to switch on your rational brain. With the growth in popularity of emotional intelligence, as a fairly new branch of psychology, its definition can be found in various theories and models. I'm sharing with you a definition influenced by a few theories, and mainly popularised by Daniel Goleman's 1995 book *Emotional Intelligence*. Daniel Goleman, considered one of the world's leading authorities on the subject, explains emotional intelligence as having five components:

1. *Self-awareness:* The ability to recognise and understand your personal moods, emotions and drives, as well as their effect on others. Self-awareness depends on your ability to monitor your own emotional state and to correctly identify and name your emotions.

2. *Self-regulation:* The ability to control or redirect disruptive impulses and moods and the propensity to suspend judgement and to think before acting.

3. *Internal motivation:* A passion to work for internal reasons that go beyond external rewards such as money and status.

4. *Empathy:* The ability to understand the emotional makeup of other people and treat people according to their emotional reactions.

5. *Social skills:* The proficiency to manage relationships, build networks, find common ground and build rapport.

Emotional intelligence is a part of you that affects every aspect of your life. Understanding the root causes of your emotions and how to use them can help you to effectively identify who you are and how you interact with others. When working on this, remembering that your emotions are not the 'enemy' is important. Your emotions contain valuable information that, if used properly, can help you make sound decisions.

Much is still to be learned about the human brain and how it works but for you to become a customer service professional, remember that understanding and using your emotional intelligence is something that your employers and customers value highly – and something that will ultimately make your job easier and less stressful.

Using and improving your emotional intelligence

Let's look at the five components of emotional intelligence and how you can transfer knowledge in this area into your role as a customer service provider.

Self-awareness

Ask yourself this question every day before you step into your workplace: How are you feeling and how could those feelings affect your behaviour?

When we consider our state of mind, we are able to then consider if we need to change it. (Similar ideas are also covered in the 'A is for Attitude' chapter.)

Self-regulation

Once you are able to identify your mood and how it makes you behave, the next step is to consider how that mood may affect everyone you come in contact with. Your negative mood will impact negatively on others and make your day just that little bit more difficult. Your positive and happy mood will not necessarily have exactly the opposite effect – it may be appreciated by some but others may consider it disruptive and irritating.

Self-regulation in your role as a customer service provider requires you to act in a way that makes your customers feel most comfortable. Being able to regulate your behaviour is vital when you are serving angry, upset or confused customers. You may be feeling like walking away, yelling back at them or suggesting that they are the world's greatest egg-shaped idiot – but if you act on your emotions, regret will soon follow (and the job hunting will likely begin).

Internal motivation

To become a customer service professional, you need to be clear on why you should bother. I lost sight of this while I was working in the bank and it not only changed my behaviour but also had a negative impact on my health and my general feeling about work. I believe that tapping in to what motivates you to work in a customer service role is so important that I've devoted a whole chapter to this very component (see the 'I is for Internal Motivation' chapter).

Empathy

Empathy is your ability to consider things from another person's point of view. It is often termed as 'putting yourself in someone else's shoes'. Some of us find empathy quite natural and others not so easily. If you find it difficult to have empathy for your customers – especially those who are being rude or abusive – ask yourself this one question: Why is this customer behaving this way?

The fact is, you won't really know exactly why a customer is using certain behaviours. But you can save yourself a lot of frustration by remembering that every customer you interact with has more going on in their life than you could ever be fully aware of. Your role is not to judge; your role is to be considerate and provide excellent service.

To help you get started, think about these possible reasons customers may need your empathy:

- They just received a call from the doctor and it was bad news.
- They are in pain – emotional or physical.
- They need your product or service but fear they can't afford it.
- They are afraid of looking stupid by not knowing everything you know.
- They just saw or read something that made them angry, upset or sad.
- They are running late for another appointment.
- They have no or a low level of self-awareness and self-regulation.

Social skills

When you master the preceding four components of emotional intelligence, this fifth component is going to be much easier.

> Customer service professionals develop their social skills because they know their ability to interact with people in a friendly and social manner is a vital step in helping their customers feel valued.

Here are a few examples of excellent social skills when interacting with customers:

- make the effort to say hello or smile when you see customers
- seek and use customers' names
- remember and enquire about customers' special life events
- maintain eye contact when you are listening to customers
- be mindful of a customer's special needs – for example, offer a seat or move to a quieter location
- apologise for delays
- be honest at all times – if you don't know, it's okay to say so
- avoid talking over or interrupting a customer.

Emotional intelligence action

We often go about our workdays unaware of how events can make us feel and act. To become more self-aware, try this activity during a workday:

1. Set an alarm for every hour on the hour.
2. When the alarm goes off, write down one word that explains how you are feeling.
3. At the end of the day, review the list.
4. Think back on your day and determine how those feelings may have made you act.
5. Think about whether you can identify any commonalities between events and your feelings.

The preceding process helps you identify strong negative emotions which may need to be calmed after work, but also shows you that, during the course of a day at work, you also will have had positive emotions. We often forget the positive things because one strong negative event can override many positive ones. Focus on the positive and seek ways to overcome the negative.

F

IS FOR FUN

This is the real secret of life – to be completely engaged with what you are doing in the here and now. And instead of calling it work, realise it is play.

ALAN W WATTS

Walt Disney is credited with creating the happiest place on Earth – Disneyland. Sure, he may have had a great marketing team who promoted Disneyland as such, but along with the Disney characters, the rides, the sights and the sounds you can experience at Disneyland, Walt knew that it was his employees who held the power to give his customers the best possible experience of his business.

Sir Richard Branson could be considered as a 'modern-day Walt Disney'. He strongly believes that how you treat your employees determines whether they provide a level of service that has their customers coming back – and bringing all of their friends and family with them.

You might not realise it, but having fun at work is one of the best things you can do for yourself, those you work with and every customer you interact with. But fun means different things to different people. Let me explain …

My husband thinks 'fun' is driving his MX5 race car around a race track at speeds that make my arm hairs stand on end – I know this for sure because I went in the car with him, once. I think 'fun' is getting in my everyday car and visiting new places, wandering through markets and shops and coming across unique things to take home. One of my closest friends finds it fun when she, her husband and their kids get on their bikes and go for long rides together. I have other friends who love water skiing, running, reading books, fixing things, watching movies or live music events – and the list goes on. You too will have what you consider your own kind of fun.

The rules of workplace fun

Fun at work comes with conditions, but then so does every type of fun we have. For my husband to have fun car racing, he has to hold a racing licence and abide by the rules of the track. For me to have fun on my driving/wandering/shopping trips, I need a driver's licence and must pay for any purchases using the rules of that business. For my friend and her family to have fun on their bikes, they have to wear helmets and abide by the road rules.

Workplaces have rules about fun too. One person's joke, funny story or picture, for example, could be another person's insult. I know, it sounds like I'm being the 'fun police', but you don't want your best intention of creating some fun by sharing a joke or story to become a situation where you have to apologise for causing offense. This can cause you stress – and all that hard work of smiling and laughing will be undone.

The benefits of fun

A wonderful side effect of fun is that the simple act of smiling is great for your health. And using humour and laughter has great health benefits too.

The health benefits of smiling

Here's what a simple smile can do for you and those around you:

- *Lowered heart rate:* smiling slows the heart rate, relaxes the body and temporarily reduces blood pressure. People who smile and laugh often are less likely to develop heart disease.
- *Reduced stress:* smiling releases endorphins that help to deactivate stress hormones.
- *Improved mood:* even if you start with a 'fake' smile, in as little as six seconds your 'fake' smile can take over your whole face and, before you know it, you will feel happier.

But be prepared; sometimes smiling can cause another side effect. You might laugh. Laughter is also really good for you – so good that it's used in the health industry as medicine.

The healing power of humour

In November 2011, I had the great pleasure of presenting at an aged care providers national conference and the other guest speaker at the conference was Dr Peter Spitzer, general practitioner, medical director and co-founder of The Humour Foundation (also known as The Clown Doctors). The Humour Foundation does amazing work. They provide a team of people who dress up as clown doctors and administer a very special brand of medicine. The medicine is free and it's called laughter.

Research conducted around the world has provided evidence of the physiological and psychological benefits of laughter to health and wellbeing.

And according to research summarised on www.humourfoundation.com.au, the benefits of laughter are many. Laughter:

- relaxes the muscles
- helps the immune system
- reduces pain
- reduces stress
- helps to promote a positive outlook
- helps promote a feeling of well being
- has a positive effect on the cardiovascular and respiratory system, similar to exercise.

Research on www.humourfoundation.com.au also highlights that humour that is based on caring and empathy:

- creates bonds between people
- is nourishing
- helps people cope with difficult situations
- is supportive

- gives people cognitive control
- provides diversion.

Check out the Humour Foundation's website to find out more about research into the benefits of laughter.

As you can see from the preceding benefits, even in what could be considered the most distressing of workplaces – hospitals with very sick children – fun not only is useful but also encouraged.

Use this knowledge to bring a sense of perspective to your role as a customer service person.

> **The simple act of smiling at your customers can effectively change how they feel.**

Why sometimes you have to say NO to fun

One of the wonderful things about working in a customer service role is that you get to interact with and meet different people. Some of those people will share the same sense of humour as you, and not only can this make for fun interactions but you will also enjoy helping these people and they will enjoy engaging with you. As a customer service professional though, you will have to be mindful of not letting those customers take up more of your time than is necessary and not becoming unprofessional.

I have had customers invite me to social functions outside of work and bring me gifts to show their appreciation for my level of service. As nice as this may seem, and even though the intentions are good, you must be mindful of the business's policies regarding these types of gratitudes.

Many workplaces have strict rules regarding the acceptance of customer gifts and attendance at after-hour customer functions, so make sure you find out what your workplace deems as suitable.

As with having fun with your customers, having fun with your co-workers also has guidelines. Your workplaces will have policies around what is considered practical and suitable activities that are aimed at generating smiles in the workplace – for example, Codes of Conduct and Occupational Health & Safety guidelines.

Being employed to do work we enjoy and with people who are a joy to work with really does make a difference. This has not always been the case in my career and understandably not everybody has the good fortune or the opportunity to gain employment in a job that they deeply enjoy. In those situations, it is even more important that you make the time to have fun outside of work. Whenever possible, seek to do things that make you happy and you will at the very least arrive at work feeling happy.

Fun action

Throughout my career I've seen wonderful examples of how customer service teams can have fun while being mindful and respectful of the diversity of everyone at work, including the customers.

Consider the following as ways to bring fun to your workplace:

- arrange a birthday cake for staff members' birthdays
- play uplifting music as staff arrive at meetings
- organise a staff social club for end-of-year celebrations
- run competitions – for example, ask staff to bring in baby photos and then guess who is who
- prepare morning tea to share with the team
- bring in your favourite books and create a staff share library
- support a charity – for example, Red Nose Day, Jeans for Genes Day or Movember
- share your culture – for example, make or bring your favourite food for others to try
- raise funds for a local cause
- seek staff input to create fun activities.

G

IS FOR GENERATION GAPS

My generation is not strong.
My grandfather fought in World War II.
I had a panic attack during the series
finale of Breaking Bad.

COMEDIAN MATT DONAHER

No doubt at some point you have heard words similar to these:

- 'Things were much better in my day.'
- 'He/she is so out of touch.'
- 'He/she is so old-fashioned.'
- 'Today's generation are so …'

Perhaps you have even spoken words similar to these. These statements are usually attributed to those of a different generation to the speaker.

The truth about the gaps

The term 'generation gap' is used to describe the different values and attitudes of people born into different generations. Since the 1960s, the term has been used to describe the clashes that one age group has with another in different settings. The role of a customer service provider usually places you in one such setting – where the different generations have to intermingle and deal with each other's ways of thinking and acting.

In general, we think of a generation being about 25 years long – from the birth of one person to the birth of their child. We also generally accept that the length of a generation in earlier periods of history was closer to 20 years (when humans mated younger and life expectancies were shorter).

The Western world has gone a step further to classify and name particular generations in relation to world events and advancements that were taking place over a particular time frame. The model is very useful for understanding that people can be quite different according to when (in history) they were born, especially because of the historical and cultural influences that occurred during their childhood and teenage years.

Of course, the framework for generations is very loose, not scientific at all, and has no single point of origin or founding theorist. And the idea of characterising an entire generation – that is, tens of millions of people – in such a sweeping way is somewhat unusual. Nevertheless, fundamental correlations can be seen between time of birth, society and the culture, on which premises the model is based.

The terms for each generation and the decades they relate to are also different across the world. This is one example:

1. *Baby boomers (1946–1960):* baby boomers are those born during the 'baby boom' that followed World War II. Baby boomers

mostly lived safe from war and serious hardship; grew up mostly in two-parent families and, more often than not, enjoyed economic prosperity. They held strong opinions on equality, freedom, the environment and peace, and were comfortable protesting and challenging authority.

2. *Generation X (1961–1980):* According to Oxford Dictionaries (blog.oxforddictionaries.com) the term 'generation X' can be traced back to as early as the 1950s, when it was used more broadly to refer to a 'generation of young people about whose future there is uncertainty'. It came into widespread use after the release of the 1991 novel *Generation X* by Doug Coupland. Members of Generation X are often described as cynical or disaffected; however, through being brought up in an era of technological and social change, they are often more open and accepting of diversity.

3. *Generation Y (1981–1999):* Generation Y was simply the next logical term to follow Generation X. These guys are totally comfortable with digital and their ability to multi-task is something to behold. Opportunities appear to be everywhere for this generation, but this requires them to have the ability to juggle school, sports training, dance class, computer games and other social interests, all while sending selfies, typing text messages and updating Facebook. They have also grown up with a 'screen' view of terrorism and violence like no other generation before them.

4. *Generation Z or the new millennials (2000–current):* Gen Z is the generation of children born after 2000. They were practically born with a screen in their hands and the uncanny ability to program all manner of digital devices. Generation Z are highly connected,

living in an age of high-tech communication, technology-driven lifestyles and prolific use of social media. At this stage, a lot of what we think we know about Generation Z is inferred, and only time will tell how they will engage in our workforces and ultimately shape our world.

Remember: the generation gap is really more of a perception than an issue. Every generation has examples of success, laziness, drive, determination, motivation and inconsistency. Putting labels on people in relation to the generation they were born into is shallow and is not how a customer service professional operates.

How perceived generation gaps may impact your role

According to Australia's Department of Human Services (www.human-services.gov.au), from 1 July 2017, the qualifying age for the Age Pension will increase from 65 years to 65 years and six months. The qualifying age will then increase by six months every two years, reaching 67 years by 1 July 2023. This means, by 2023, workplaces could be made up of people from all four of the current generations – Generation Z will be moving into work while the last of the baby boomers will be yet to reach the retirement age. When people who work together share the same values and attitudes, communication and other dynamics typically go smoother. When multiple generations are working together, each generation brings their own style, values, and attitudes and this could create tension and other issues. (I cover this further in the 'T is for Team Work' chapter.)

For co-workers from different generations to work together in harmony, we need to view the gap as something that is less of a problem and more of an opportunity. In reality, both in the workplace and at home, lots of reciprocity occurs between the generations, especially once they come to know and understand one another, even just a little.

> As a customer service provider, you will be required to interact with customers from a range of generations, so it's important for you to consider the differences and use that knowledge to communicate in a way that builds trust and shows respect.

Addressing people from different generations

I am often asked how customer service providers should address customers who are much older than themselves. You will find that some older customers will be happy for you to use their first name and others may find that too familiar and would prefer to be addressed as Mr/Mrs/Ms. The same concern with how to address a person may happen for customers with a professional title – for example, Dr, Father, Rabbi, Sir or Madam.

The simplest and most effective way to handle the uncertainty is to ask. If ever you are in doubt, always ask the customer how they would like to be addressed. If you make a mistake, apologise. If the customer is someone you will be interacting with regularly, take note of what they prefer to be called and make a record of their preference where other staff will also be aware. You may think the name they prefer is overly formal and perhaps you may feel a little uncomfortable but this will pass.

Generally, most customers will give you permission to use their first name but don't assume and think that will be everyone, or you could inadvertently cause offence and miss your opportunity to delight.

Generation gaps action

In order to better communicate with and provide help to customers born in different generations from you, take the time to learn more about what was influencing the culture as they were growing up.

Identify two people either in your workplace or in your private life who were born into a generation different from yours and ask the following questions.

When you were 16:

- What was the greatest technology available?
- What did you do in your spare time?
- What was your favourite book or movie?
- What did you want to be or do when you grew up?
- Who did you consider a good role model of the time?
- What was customer service like when you were a customer?

These questions can tell you a lot about a person and give you an understanding of how they grew up and what they valued. The more you understand about the different generations, the more you can tailor your service to suit customers from different generations.

H

IS FOR HANDLING COMPLAINTS

Your most unhappy customers are
your greatest source of learning.

BILL GATES

Bill Gates was correct in the preceding quote (and, remember, he made quite a good living when he developed his products with Microsoft). If a business doesn't embrace complaints and make it easy for customers to share their concerns, customers will take their business elsewhere.

If your customers have no choice but to do business with you, this can create an equally bad situation – they will stay and remind you just how unhappy they are, constantly. The truth is, if a customer isn't telling the business what they don't like, they will be telling someone. Statistics from the 1980s showed that unhappy customers will tell 8 to 16 people about their dissatisfaction. Can you imagine what that statistic is today, considering how easy it is to voice our displeasure via social media?

> We can't please all of the customers all of time but we can learn the skills to make it easier.

Why are customers so cranky?

Over the past 30-plus years of my career, I have noticed that Australian consumers are becoming more demanding. Not only do customers young and old seem more willing to complain, but also the behaviour some people use to communicate their unhappiness can be quite concerning. What has happened to create this increase in cranky customers and complaints?

Here are my thoughts:

- The internet allows people to research before making purchases, thus giving them a sense of control when they interact with the business. They know what they want and they want it now, and they are prepared to challenge you with their insights.
- Online shopping has meant a dramatic downturn in the level of face-to-face and instant customer service from a person. Customers, although pleased with 24/7 shopping, want a human to speak to when things go wrong, and by then they are already upset.
- Social media allows customers to complain and share their complaints with a worldwide audience. Some people use those

opinions to give them the courage to seek a better deal or push for something they wouldn't normally ask for.

- An increase in reality television programs that show examples of people behaving badly. I wonder if these shows have helped us forget that bad behaviour has consequences and it's not okay to be demanding, rude or inconsiderate of the rights and feelings of the customer service provider. I wonder if we have forgotten that reality TV is rarely a view of reality.

The desire for face-to-face and immediate customer service can also in part be determined by the generation the customer was born into. I'm Generation X and I remember when the only way you could purchase goods was to visit the business and interact with a person.

> **One thing is consistent across all generations: a customer complaint occurs when the expectation of the customer has not been met.**

The job with no complaints

When I was job seeking after I left the bank, I thought hard about what type of industry I would enjoy working in. I considered all the things I didn't want to do in a job and all the things I enjoyed doing. It became very clear to me that the one thing I disliked the most was dealing with what I considered difficult people. At this time, I had lost my ability to empathise with people and I realised this was because my final years in the bank saw me dealing with lots of complaints – complaints from the staff I managed, complaints from my managers about targets not being met and, of course, customer complaints.

So, with that in mind I thought it would be best if I worked in a job with *only* polite, friendly and happy people. And, yes, I really did search for that job. Let me save you some time if you too are wondering where that job is. No such job exists. Any job with people involved means there is a chance of disagreements, complaints or conflict. Getting along with everyone would leave us with no room to improve, no new and interesting insights and, yes, the world would be boring if we were all the same.

Learning how to handle difficult situations is easier and less stressful than trying to avoid them. To help with this, let's first look at the main things people complain about.

The three Ps customers complain about

Businesses succeed when they have identified and met the needs of their customers. Customers will decide if they want to access what the business has to offer by assessing the three Ps:

1. *Product*: the cost and suitability of the items or services that a business sells or provides.
2. *Process*: the steps in place for the customer to access or receive the products.
3. *People*: the employees of the business and how they interact with the customer.

Depending on the size or type of business you work for, you may have little or no control over the products or processes the business has in place. When you agree with the complaint a customer brings to you, these business products or processes can require you to act in a way contrary to how you feel.

I experienced this in my own career – when the bank I worked with introduced automatic teller machines (ATMs) into branches in regional Victoria in the early 1990s. At this time, our elderly customers were in the habit of queuing up at the front door at 9.30 am (opening time) every Thursday fortnight to withdraw their pensions. As we opened the doors, they would all file in together, happily chatting away to each other and the staff. We would process their transactions and then this sea of senior citizens would move off to the next destination on their agenda.

And then the ATMs were put in the wall, and staff were expected to 'guide' all customers out of the branch and on to the footpath to introduce them to the large metal monster that required a secret code, made beeping noises and spat out money.

And so the complaints and questions from our elderly customers began – for example:

- 'It's way too dangerous for me to stand on the street with cash in my hand.'
- 'You will lose your jobs if we use this machine.'
- 'I can't remember a four-digit number.'
- 'What if the money blows away before I can get it in my purse/wallet?'
- 'What if the machine gives me the wrong amount of money?'
- 'What if someone steals my plastic card?'
- 'What if my card doesn't come back out?'
- 'I don't want to stand on the street; I want to talk to the lovely staff.'

Most of our staff, myself included, agreed with our elderly customers. We couldn't say that to them but, in our hearts, we believed that some if not all of their objections and concerns were valid. Staff shared these concerns with management and included our major concern at the top of the list – would we lose our jobs? The managers collated the feedback and elevated the concerns and complaints to their superiors.

Did the ATMs go away? No. Did customers eventually embrace them – including a majority of the elderly? Yes. Did the staff appreciate that their concerns were heard? Yes. Management addressed staff concerns and provided the training and time to help both customers and staff embrace new technology. Some staff and customers needed more time to adapt than others but, as we now know, technology will keep evolving and businesses need to adapt to the needs of their customers or risk losing them.

There may be times in your career when, like me, you are on the side of the complaining customer. Customer service professionals listen to those complaints and offer empathy but always present themselves as a professional representative of the business. If you hold strong moral or ethical views about what the business requests of you, professionally address this directly with your manager.

When you hear customer complaints, you should record them so the businesses can assess if there is an opportunity for their products or processes to improve. Most businesses have a customer complaint process, which you should follow. Keep the three Ps in mind when a customer complains but remember: it's how you communicate with the customers that will determine if they leave you feeling respected and valued. You have 100 per cent control over the third P – your people skills.

> Your customer is complaining to you because they believe you can help – that's a compliment. It may be 'wrapped in barbed-wire' but it is a compliment.

Is the customer always right?

You may have heard this statement before: 'The customer is always right.' If not explained correctly, however, this statement can be misleading and can make customer service providers feel powerless. They may feel they are left with little or no confidence to help an unhappy customer. Earlier on in my customer service career, I found it particularly difficult to listen to customers who would embellish the truth, make things up, have no idea what they were talking about or simply lie. Why would they do this? Why would they be so rude or arrogant? To get what they wanted. With this is mind, let me tell you that not all of your customers will always be right.

Think of a time when you had to interact with a customer who was wrong. How did that interaction make you feel? Maybe you felt annoyed, frustrated, angry or nervous. This is only a problem if you are unable to control those feelings. You may want to yell back at the customer, tell them they are wrong or simply walk away. All of those options will cause you more problems but, at the time, they may seem like the best thing to do.

When we act on our emotions, we may do or say things we later regret or we may miss the opportunity to do or say things that could have been helpful at the time.

> The customer may not be right, but it is not our job to prove him/her wrong.

How to take the LEAD

The feeling of powerlessness can be overwhelming when you are in the midst of upset customers. Your ability to control your reactions (see the 'E is for Emotional Intelligence' chapter) to these situations is paramount to you not only helping the customers but also helping yourself. To help you in those times, I recommend using my LEAD process. LEAD outlines the four steps you can take to help you take charge professionally when dealing with a difficult, demanding or complaining customer.

I used the word 'LEAD' because it gives me a feeling of control. I lead customers to a more rational and less emotional mental state, and the four steps in the process also have the effect of helping me to remain calm and rational throughout.

The aim of the LEAD process is to reduce your customer's emotional state from an irrational 10 down to a more rational 3 or below, and to do this before you commence negotiating or offering solutions. Take the LEAD and help your emotional client through to a calmer place where they feel respected and ready to listen to you.

L – Listen

When a customer is complaining, annoyed or upset, you need to actively listen. Active listening means giving your customer 100 per cent of your attention. Ignore outside distractions and focus on what the customer is saying. Read their body language, listen to their tone of voice and take notes if appropriate. Give your customer permission to continue by nodding and using eye contact as well as offering verbal prompts such as, 'Uh huh', 'I see' or 'Go on'. Unless absolutely necessary, do not interrupt an upset customer. This will annoy them further – and trying to solve the problem before they have finished speaking will make things worse.

E – Empathise

Empathy, which is considering your customer's point of view or putting yourself in their shoes, is the skill of an emotionally intelligent person. Empathy does not mean you agree with the complaint or the behaviour. You are simply showing you understand why they are upset or angry. While you are listening you can display empathy with eye contact and nodding but, if appropriate, you can offer your words as well – for example, 'I understand you are annoyed. Please go on.', 'Yes, that would be very frustrating. Please tell me more.', 'I'm sorry you feel this way and I am glad you are telling me as I am here to help.'

A – Acknowledge

Once you have gathered all the information, confirm by repeating or paraphrasing what you have heard. You may find that what they are saying and what you heard are different. More active listening and possibly some open and closed questions (see the 'L is for Listening' chapter for more on this) will help to clarify and again shows that you respect your customer and that you are listening. While the customer is listening to you, this is helping to calm them as it is engaging their rational brain (cortex) and slowing their flow of emotions.

D – Decide

Once the emotion has been calmed, you are now communicating with a rational person. If you have to tell a customer 'no' or that what they want is not possible, it is much easier for them to hear this in a rational state. You may need to refer for assistance or you may be able to solve the problem yourself, but always give the customer clear and achievable solutions and never forget to thank them. You are thanking them for bringing the problem or complaint to you and allowing you the chance to help them.

Reasons customer service professionals choose to LEAD

With practise, LEAD becomes second nature. I use it without even thinking and from the following feedback I've received from customer service professionals, it clearly works across various industries. Here's what they had to say:

- 'LEAD makes it so much easier. I know what to do and that alone makes me less anxious.' (Pharmacy assistant)
- 'I used LEAD the other day and the customer ended up thanking me before I had even got to D – she realised she was going over the top and apologised straight away.' (Awning installer)
- 'I took me quite a few practices but I finally can do this with ease and it's so wonderful when a customer says sorry for their bad behaviour.' (Water industry call centre operator)
- 'Although LEAD doesn't work with every upset customer, it works every time to keep me calm.' (School administrator)
- 'I was pretty good at L and E but I had never bothered to repeat what the customer had said (A). It made a hugely positive difference to the outcome.' (Clothing retailer)
- 'A good day is when I get to use the LEAD process. It's not great that we have unhappy customers but I look forward to helping turn them into an advocate for our business.' (Employment consultant)
- 'LEAD stops me from interrupting, which I didn't realise was the worst thing to do with an unhappy customer.' (Medical receptionist)

- 'I used LEAD last week and the customer still left in a bad mood. I thought I had failed but she rang me the next day and apologised for her behaviour and said I was wonderful for listening to her and was sorry for leaving in a huff.' (Accounting practice receptionist)

When not to LEAD

On any given day you may find yourself interacting with a customer who is abusive, violent, offensive or threatening. In those situations it is important that you abide by the safety standards of your organisation, which in most cases will be to cease the communication. I cover this more completely in the 'W is for Worst Case Scenarios' chapter. LEAD is not recommended as these situations require a focus on safety – yours, your co-workers and your customers.

Remember – LEAD is useful for the everyday customer complaint but should not be tried in any situation you feel violated, threatened or abused.

Extra tips for handling complaints

If you still require some more help when dealing with complaints, consider the following:

- Whether in your mind the complaint is justified or unjustified, your response requires the same level of professional respect. In the eyes of the customer, only one type of complaint exists – justified.
- Record complaints and review them with the team. You will be able to quickly identify re-occurring problems, make improvements and share best practices.

- Stay away from responding to bait, and don't lose your temper. If both you and your customer end up in a shouting match, or worse, you are unlikely to solve anything.
- Offer alternatives and, when you cannot provide what the customer wants, remind them what you can do. For example, you could say something like, 'I understand you're frustrated that I can't complete the job today, but I will call you when it has been completed and keep you up to date.'
- Customers are not the opposition. Customers only know what they want and it may not be what you can do. Your job is to educate your customers, not to point out you know more. Respect their position and don't talk down to them.
- Customers are not attacking you personally, but may have become very frustrated with a situation they cannot control. As a result, the quality of their normal communication can take a severe dip.
- Understand that a person raising their voice often believes this is their best and possibly only way to be heard and get what they want. You don't have to agree with what they are saying or how they are saying it, you have to remain professional and take the LEAD.

The good news is that not all customers are difficult. In fact, most customers are pleasant, happy, understanding and willing to work with you to achieve the best outcomes for all the stakeholders of your business.

Handling complaints action

LEAD requires practise. When first starting to use it, don't rely on your memory to complete the four steps in the process. Write out the LEAD process and place it where you can see it daily. Eventually the steps will become more natural and you will find it easy to LEAD your unhappy customers to a calmer emotional state.

I

IS FOR INTERNAL MOTIVATION

Whether you think you can
or think you can't – you're right.

HENRY FORD, FOUNDER OF THE FORD MOTOR COMPANY

Ask yourself: what will you get out of becoming a customer service professional? It's likely pretty clear why the business and the customers would like you to take up the challenge, but unless you have identified why you personally should make the effort, you probably won't bother. Internal motivation is what you will need to not only become but also remain a customer service professional. This is a project you will need to work on for the entirety of your career, so being able to sustain the focus and the desire means getting crystal clear on what benefits you will achieve.

Why bother becoming a customer service professional?

From the moment a customer service professional enters the workplace, they are focused on what's best for the customer – every customer. This takes effort. Some days this focus can leave them feeling tired, frustrated or even angry, and it's exactly on those days that they remind themselves why they are doing it. They remind themselves of their prize – the reason that goes beyond getting paid and doing what the boss wants.

You have to identify what your prize/s will be. You have to find **WIIFM: W**hat's **I**n **I**t **F**or **M**e?

I ask attendees in my training sessions to get clear on their WIIFM in relation to becoming and remaining a customer service professional. This is a personal question, because everyone's motivation to be better than just a good customer service provider may be different. You may find it quite easy to answer the question or you may struggle. Some of my training attendees have to dig deep to identify why they should make the extra effort. I have had some attendees even take a moment to re-consider if working as a customer service provider is really for them. (If this is you, check out the 'R is for Reality Check' chapter for some help.)

Customer service professionals know that they receive more than their wage when they exceed their customers' expectations.

> Providing service to others is actually quite selfish. You see, when we provide a service to others and we do it so well that the customer's expectation is exceeded, amazing things can happen to you.

Benefits of becoming a customer service professional

As already mentioned, your WIIFM will be personal, but may incorporate some of the following benefits:

- more compliments
- fewer complaints
- increased job satisfaction
- increased personal satisfaction
- more able to leave work at work – no longer worrying about work at home
- employer looking to you for customer service strategies
- increased mentoring opportunities with customer service staff
- more thank you phone calls, cards and emails from delighted customers
- more interest from other employers who want to hire you
- increased confidence when dealing with angry or upset customers
- reached and exceeded sales targets
- more understanding of the great value you have in your organisation
- improved communication with co-workers
- reduced fear of the difficult customer interactions
- more time available to do the things you enjoy – both in and out of work
- increased enjoyment of work – it is much more fun
- reduced anxiety about asking for help
- more energy for your family when you get home

- more confidence in putting your customer service improvement ideas forward to your employer
- reduced stress.

The preceding list was created from comments made by existing customer service professionals, with the final item something that every single customer service professional had on their list. They know that minimising stress at work will have a positive effect in other areas of their life as well.

Imagine what it could be like to:

- receive more compliments than complaints
- have the skills to turn complaints into a compliments
- finish work and going home smiling
- have the energy to interact positively with your family and friends
- receive letters, cards and genuine thanks for your great service
- show a prospective employer these letters and cards
- work in a team of positive and helpful people
- have your employer ask you for advice regarding customer service issues.

Great news! You can stop imagining because this book gives you everything you need to make it happen.

Internal motivation action

Think of three things you personally will gain from being a customer service professional. Be honest – if you don't have any personal rewards for taking the steps to become and remain a customer service professional, chances are you won't bother to make the effort or, if you do, you won't be able to sustain this effort in the long term.

Take the time to write down your three internal motivators:

1. _____

2. _____

3. _____

J

IS FOR JUGGLING

*If you want something done,
ask a busy person.*

BENJAMIN FRANKLIN

In the quote above, Benjamin Franklin was suggesting that busy people know how to get things done. They are motivated by the opportunity to meet deadlines and have the ability to complete many tasks, often simultaneously. They are like a juggler who not only keeps multiple balls in the air, but also spins a plate on one foot and works a hula hoop, all at the same time. How much practise – and how many broken plates – do you think it took to be able to do that while also smiling at the people watching?

Succeeding in a role that has an element of customer interaction – especially if your role is to be the first point of contact for customers

– means you will at times have to be able to juggle and spin plates and work that hula hoop too. Your ability to prioritise and complete tasks in line with organisational standards while also attending to the needs of your customers is part and parcel of many workplace roles.

> **The true challenge is not just getting everything done; it's getting everything done like a customer service professional.**

Remember – when you know your natural behavioural style you will find it easier to determine the tasks that you can do easily, with little or no effort, and those that will take more of your energy. Self-awareness is key to you being able to complete multiple tasks and meet deadlines – so if you haven't read the 'B is for Behavioural Styles' chapter, I recommend you do so now.

Meeting the needs of multiple customers at the same time

How to meet the needs of multiple customers is such a great question because it tells me one very important thing. Those who ask this question are already on the road to becoming customer service professionals. They know that every customer deserves the same amount of attention so when they are confronted by two or more customers at the same time, they want to know how to provide superior service to them all.

The answer to this common dilemma lies in your ability to juggle like a professional. Professional jugglers make throwing and catching multiple balls at the same time seem like it is the easiest thing in the world to do. Most customers will respond positively when you show you are calm and in control and that you recognise and value their needs. If you work in a team of customer service professionals, you can help each other when these situations arise. One person gets the phone, for example, while one person serves the walk-in customer and you get to finalise your existing customer's transaction.

If you are on your own, however, your ability to prioritise will help but remember: it's your body language and tone of voice that will tell customers how you are feeling and what your attitude is. Consider the following:

- A nod and eye contact can let waiting customers know that you value them and will be with them soon.
- If you need to answer a phone, seek permission from your face-to-face customer or let the call go through to the message bank. If you do answer the call, advise the customer on the phone you will be with them shortly and ask permission to place them on hold or to call them back. If you're going to call them back, give a realistic time frame and make sure you call them back within that time frame.
- If some customers are becoming annoyed at having to wait, use your body language and tone of voice to confirm that you are in control and that you will be with them as soon possible.

What ducks teach us about being great jugglers

Think of a duck on a pond. Ducks glide across the water with seemingly little or no effort. But underneath the water, what we don't see is that their duck feet are doing all the work to move them forward and to keep afloat. Ducks appear to us to be calm; with no obvious signs of stress, they get from point A to point B with what seems like little or no effort at all.

Customer service professionals go about their days like ducks. When we let our customers know that we are stressed, busy or time poor, we have shifted the focus onto us. Practise controlling your body language and tone of voice when you have many things to juggle. Be a duck, a duck that juggles.

> **Customers are not there to help you; you are there to help them.**

The four Ds to beat procrastination

The reason some of us may struggle to get everything done is our inability to prioritise tasks and make decisions. This can affect the level of service we provide to our customers, because the idea of stopping what we are doing to provide service to our customers can become frustrating, and our body language can come across to customers as if they are an interruption and not welcome.

The four Ds help me when I'm feeling overwhelmed and need to be focused on my customers:

- *Do it now:* handle the worse things first. We create more stress and anxiety and waste more time and energy over the things we least like to do. Stop procrastinating, make a plan and move forward.
- *Deactivate digital distractions:* set and stick to digital-free time. Turn off email notifications, put your phone and devices on silent or turn them off. Unless required for emergency contact, devices will only distract you from getting things done.

- *Deadlines:* set and stick to them. And if you have deadlines, remember to pass them on to others as well. Don't let someone else's lack of planning short circuit your deadlines.
- *Delegate:* don't waste time doing things that somebody else can do, especially if they can do them better than you. Avoid falling into the trap of, 'It's quicker and easier to do it myself'.

How to survive peak periods

Peak periods are the times when your business tasks and customer needs increase. This can be related to things like public holidays, sales, promotional events and staff shortages. These times require customer service professionals to work in top gear and really bring their 'duck skills' to work.

I remember very clearly the peak periods in the bank. They were always in the lead-up to a public holiday and they would mean queues out the door, grumpy and time-poor customers and staff feeling overworked and sometimes under appreciated. I once found a co-worker hiding out during her lunch break in the stationery room. She was sitting on a stepladder, eating her sandwich and reading a book. I asked her why she didn't just have her lunch in the staff room and her reply was, 'I'm sick of people'. I understood, closed the door and gave her some peace.

Sometimes that's exactly what you are going to need to do: find a quiet place during a break and take a moment just for you. Providing consistently excellent service during peak times can be very tiring. Most businesses will have peak periods so make sure you know when to expect them and take the time to consider what you can do to recharge your service batteries – and don't forget to support your co-workers when they need time out too.

Further tips to survive the peak periods:

- *Avoid late nights and get some sleep*: having customers make demands of us is hard enough when we are alert, but being tired makes this harder.
- *Don't rely on your memory*: take notes and create lists. Record the tasks you need to do and tick them off as you complete them. Peak periods often mean interruptions and if you rely on your memory to complete customer requests, you're making it harder on yourself.
- *Stay hydrated*: drink water throughout the day. Water helps with keeping our minds sharp.
- *Seek help*: if things get above your abilities or you simply cannot complete all your required tasks, let your manager know and let others help you get back in control.
- *Look to help others*: peak periods may or may not have an impact on everyone in the team. Build strong workplace relationships by helping out when you're able to.
- *Reward yourself*: at the end of a peak period day or week – or however long it lasts – remember to take a moment to acknowledge how you and your team stepped up and performed like professionals.
- *Reflect*: when the peak periods are over, also take a moment to reflect. What did you do well, what could you have done better and what things could have made it easier? When we share this information with the team, peak periods can become an opportunity to share successes, learn from each other and build stronger teams.

Juggling action

A well-known story about time management uses a glass jar, rocks, stones, pebbles, sand and water to illustrate how to plan your day. The glass jar represents the time you have each day, and each item that goes into it represents an activity with a priority relative to its size, as follows:

- *Rocks:* the general idea is to fill your glass jar first with rocks. Plan each day around your most important tasks – the ones that will propel you toward achieving your goals. These represent your highest priority projects and deadlines with the greatest value. They can often also include important but not urgent tasks that move you toward your goals.

- *Pebbles:* next, fill in the space between the rocks with pebbles. These represent tasks that are urgent and important, but that contribute less to important goals. Without proper planning, these tasks often come up unexpectedly, and left unmanaged, can quickly fill your day. Working to reduce these tasks will give you more time to work toward your goals.

- *Sand:* now add sand to fill your jar. In other words, schedule urgent, but not important tasks, only after important tasks. These activities are usually routine or maintenance tasks that do not directly contribute to your goals.

- *Water:* finally, pour water into your jar. These trivial time-wasters are neither important nor urgent and take you away from working toward high-return activities and your goals.

If you commit to this approach to planning your days, you will see as time goes on that you are able to achieve more in less time. Instead of finishing things in a mad rush to meet deadlines, each day will be organised and become more productive. You will also notice yourself spending less time on activities that are of little to no value.

K

IS FOR KNOWLEDGE

Knowledge itself is power.

FRANCIS BACON

Did you know that your brain is like a filing cabinet? Over the course of our lives, we take in massive amounts of information and we then have this great filing cabinet called a brain where we can store all this information. Sometimes the information can be easily found, especially if it was collected very recently. If we haven't had to use the information for a while, however, other new information pushes old information out of the way so we may have to go searching for it until we find it. Other times, we know we have that information but no amount of searching that filing cabinet is going to help us find it. Unfortunately, unlike a well-organised and structured filing cabinet, our brains can be a bit messy. So we know the information is in there, but finding it when we need it can sometimes be impossible.

Customer service professionals keep their customer service information easily accessible by making sure their customer service knowledge is at the front of their filing cabinets – that is, their brains. They do this by seeking to learn new things and refreshing their existing knowledge regularly. In the workplace, this type of learning is called 'professional development'.

Learning while doing the job is how many first-time customer service providers are trained. On-the-job training means you will be given enough knowledge to get you started and, in some cases, may also be introduced to a workplace buddy or support person who you can go to if you have any questions. Interacting with customers without knowing how everything works can be very daunting and the different needs of each customer will often dictate the order of what you need to learn.

It would be wonderful if businesses could afford to comprehensively train new staff in not only the products and processes of the business but also the vital soft skills that will help them provide service like a customer service professional. Most businesses, however, can't afford you spending too long on learning; they will need you serving customers as soon as possible. So how can you get this information?

Improving your product and process knowledge

Gaining more understanding of your organisation's products and processes will greatly improve your customer service confidence. The following sections provide some tips on how to do so.

Increasing product knowledge

Make it your mission to read any available brochures, manuals or relevant online material (including content available on the business's intranet) about the products of the business. You may also have the opportunity to attend information sessions, either during or after hours.

Remember: you can wait for the product knowledge to be provided to you, or you can be proactive. Customer service professionals are proactive about their own professional development.

> The sooner you understand the business's products, the sooner you increase your confidence when dealing with customers.

Growing process knowledge

Processes are how things get done, and successful businesses create and review processes regularly. Processes exist to not only make things easy for the customer but also help the business run smoothly, save time, make money, recruit and retain happy staff, meet industry standards and, quite simply, keep the doors open.

Think of processes like a recipe to bake a cake. Good processes give you all the ingredients you need and the steps required for you to bake the cake, and they're designed so that any employee could also bake the cake using the same recipe. Complicated processes make it harder for the employees and the customers to understand.

> Processes are how a business runs. Good processes should make it easy for the customer to engage with a business.

Hard and soft skills

Let's now move on to the type of skills you are going to need to become and remain a customer service professional. You will need two types of skills: hard and soft skills. Hard skills are usually more tangible and easily identified, whereas as a customer service professional you also have things that are not tangible – things that you carry in your heart and mind. These are your soft skills.

The terms 'hard skills' and 'soft skills' are generally used across all industries but not everyone is clear on what those skills are referring to. The following sections provide some clarification.

Understanding hard skills

'Hard skills' is the term associated with the technical skills required for you to complete your role. Employers will often request evidence of your hard skills as a prerequisite for employment, or they may provide the necessary hard skills training when you commence the job.

Possible technical (hard) skills you may require or be willing to learn so you can successfully complete your role as a customer service provider include the following:

- first aid techniques
- languages
- machinery operation qualifications

- Microsoft Word programs (general ability)
- specific licences (for example, car or truck driver's licence)
- specific qualifications.

It's important to note that the word 'hard' in this instance does not mean that the skills are difficult to learn. Hard is used here to relate to the set steps or processes that are required to be done in the correct order for you to be deemed competent in that skill. Hard means set – not difficult.

Understanding soft skills

'Soft skills' is the term associated with a person's cluster of personal qualities, habits, attitudes and social graces. Organisations value soft skills because research suggests – and experience shows – that they can be just as important an indicator of job performance as hard skills. Employers today use various personality and behavioural testing and assessing tools to identify what soft skills candidates possess.

Examples of soft skills include the following:

- empathy
- flexibility/adaptability
- positive attitude
- problem solving abilities
- self-confidence
- stress management
- strong work ethic.

Soft here doesn't mean easy. In this usage, soft means pliable and is related to your ability to adjust those skills to provide excellent service to your different styles of customers.

Developing your hard and soft skills

A role's position or job description will tell you what hard and soft skills are required for that role. Unfortunately, not all businesses can easily provide this document and, if they can, the document may be unclear or out of date.

Successful businesses have a clear and engaging performance development program in place for all of their employees. These programs require the employee and their direct manager to openly and honestly discuss and identify not only knowledge and skills gaps but also action plans for the gaps to be filled. But again, not every workplace has a performance development program in place. If yours doesn't, many reasons for this may exist (remember the big picture). But don't let this stop you.

You can search the internet for position descriptions for roles the same as or similar to yours. They may not specify the exact skills you need, but you can take these descriptions and/or the skills listed to your employer to start a conversation about skill development. The following sections look at training in more detail.

Considering training

Now you know what skills you need, your next step is to consider which of those skills you need to improve or learn about, and then identify your training options. You can benefit from two training options: formal and informal training.

Formal training

Formal training can take many forms. It can be a traineeship or apprenticeship that includes elements of customer service, or training that your employer provides – such as e-learning, induction programs or group training. Usually this training is designed to be specific to the industry you work in. Alternatively, you may have completed your own formal customer service skills training at a TAFE or university or via a previous employer.

Formal training is specifically designed to give you the required level of customer service skills and knowledge so you can meet the standard set for your role. Formal training provided by your employer is usually in line with industry standards and may include relevant workplace policies and procedures. Formal training may be recognised across your industry and may see you achieve a specific qualification or, at the very least, receive confirmation in writing that you have achieved a desired level or standard.

Informal training

Informal training covers what you learn by doing, reading and watching – both at work and in your life. Often our best customer service learning comes from making a mistake or hearing about a mistake others have made. Indeed, being able to learn from the mistakes of others is great – it involves less impact on you and, let's be honest, you haven't got the time to make every mistake so let other people have a go too.

The internet also provides a huge source of learning material that you can access when it suits you best. Remember, however, that just because information is on the internet, it does not come with a guarantee it is true or correct. You should always check the source, and find multiple sources of the kind of information you're focusing on.

Of course, the internet provides access to more than just written text too – for example:

- *Podcasts:* audio information you can download and listen to when it best suits you. Check iTunes or Stitcher to get started.
- *YouTube:* videos of almost anything you want to learn how to master.
- *ebooks:* access to thousands of books via your favourite device. Try Kindle or Amazon if just starting out.
- *e-learning:* online programs you can complete in your own home. You can access anything from short courses in cake decorating, resume writing and car maintenance through to full business qualifications and so much more.

You have many formal and informal learning options to help you achieve your goal of becoming and remaining a customer service professional. Don't worry if you haven't had formal training or don't know how to access it. Don't let this stop you. Formal customer service training can be completed as part of your job role. As mentioned previously, this type of learning in the workplace is called 'professional development' and successful businesses either provide this or allow employees to access suitable external learning options. Employers are becoming more aware that to not only attract but also retain staff, they need to provide pro-fessional development opportunities as part of their staff employment package – so don't be afraid to discuss this with your manager.

Knowledge action

Make a list of all the hard and soft skills that you believe
you need to learn or improve on to succeed in your role.
Discuss your list with your direct manager to confirm
what actions you can put in place to develop each skill.
Put a completion date on each action and review your
progress regularly. Being proactive and organised is a sign
of a customer service professional.

L

IS FOR LISTENING

*You aren't learning anything
when you're talking.*

LYNDON B JOHNSON

I can't tell you the number of times I have heard these statements
(or similar) said by customer service providers and customers:

- 'You're not listening to me.'
- 'That's not what I said.'
- 'If you would just let me finish.'
- 'But you told me I could do that.'

Listening is an acquired and vital skill for customer service professionals.
I didn't include it in the 'C for Communication' chapter because it is so
important that it requires a chapter all on its own.

Take a moment to check out your listening skills now. What can you hear? Can you hear car noise, birds, music, a TV, machines or equipment, rain, voices? All of those sounds were happening before you stopped and concentrated on them but you may not have been aware of all of them because you weren't focused on them. Customer service professionals know that to provide a level of service that is going to delight their customers they need to be able to focus with both their eyes and their ears. They need to practise active listening.

What is active listening?

Most of us are born with the ability to hear but those who have hearing limitations are often better listeners than those who have optimal hearing. A hearing impaired person has to concentrate harder to hear what people say and that's what effective listening is all about – concentrating on what the other person has to say.

> **Active listening means giving your undivided attention with no interruptions.**

Customers respond to those who truly listen to what they have to say. If you focus on listening more than you talk, you'll quickly be identified as someone who can be trusted.

Along with talking less, we also confirm to the other person that we are actively listening with our body language – including eye contact, nods and our tone of voice – and verbal prompts. Taking notes also confirms you are listening. (Always seek permission to take notes and let your customer know when and why you will take notes.)

Mastering the art of active listening

In your role as a customer service provider, many things can make giving your undivided attention to every customer difficult. For example:

- We let our attention wander.
- We miss the real point.
- We let our emotions interfere.
- We hear something we disagree with or don't understand.
- We think ahead and miss what's being said right now.
- We are busy.

Being an active listener takes practise. Follow these three steps and you will be well on your way to being considered a great listener:

1. *Stop:* when you are about to engage with a customer, stop everything else and focus on that customer.
2. *Listen:* let the customer talk – avoid interrupting unless absolutely necessary.
3. *Paraphrase:* repeat back to the customer what you heard but using your own words. When you take a moment to repeat what a customer has said, not only are you confirming you were actively listening but doing so also allows you to check that what the customer said is what you heard.

Using questions to gain information

How do you help when the customer doesn't know what they want or how to tell you? Especially when communicating interpersonally in a diverse workplace environment, good questioning skills are critical so that the message you are receiving is accurate and complete. Active listeners use specific questioning techniques to elicit more information from speakers, and they use an effective tone to confirm they are interested and respectful of the person they are speaking with.

Questions are a great way to help you gain more information and to make a decision and help your customers further. Open questions are perfect for this situation. Closed questions, on the other hand, can be used when you need a specific 'yes/no' or fact answer.

Open questions

Using an open question stimulates thinking and discussion or responses, including opinions or feelings. Open questions pass control of the conversation from you to the customer. To get the customer talking, use leading questions that begin with the words who, what, where, when, why or how. For example:

- Who else could help us with this?
- What other ideas do you have?
- Where do you think we could improve?
- When would you prefer to be contacted?
- Why do you believe this happened?
- How did this make you feel?

You should use open questions:

- when you need more than a 'yes/no' answer
- in situations that are more complex
- when multiple choices are available
- to clarify and understand your customer's situation.

Closed questions

Closed questions usually require a one-word, yes or no answer, and effectively shut off discussion. Closed questions provide facts, allow the questioner to maintain control of the conversation, and are easy to answer. Typical leading words for closed questions are: is, can, how many, when or does.

While closed questions are not the optimum choice for active listening, at times they are necessary, and may be helpful when you are interacting with someone who speaks in a different language or who has a speech impediment. Examples of closed questions are:

- Would you like to go ahead with this purchase?
- Will you be the one using this service?
- Should I email the details to you?

You should use closed questions when:

- you need a definite or brief response
- you need clarification
- you need a confirmation
- you're in a straightforward and uncomplicated situation.

Listening action

The next time you engage with a customer, practise using open questions to learn more about their needs. Remember to paraphrase what you heard and finish your interaction with a closed question that confirms respect – for example, 'Is there anything else I can help you with today?'

M

IS FOR MYSTERY SHOPPERS

*Do what you do so well,
that they will want to see it again
and tell all of their friends.*

WALT DISNEY

During my time in banking, 'mystery shoppers' was one of the methods used to assess the sales and customer service skills of the banking staff – basically, this was where the bank engaged the services of people employed by an external company to visit the branches of the bank. These people behaved like normal customers, with the aim of collating information related to their experience.

Mystery shoppers are used across many industries. In the case of the bank, they would collect information relating to the following questions:

- Were you greeted within one minute of entering the bank?
- Did the staff member seek your name?
- Was the area clean and tidy?
- Did the staff member use your name more than three times?
- Could you hear conversations between other staff members?
- What was the name of the staff who served you?
- How long did you have to wait in a queue?
- Were you told about the special offer?

Mystery shoppers were also required to ring the branch and, again, assess various aspects of the phone conversation. For example:

- How long did the phone ring before it was answered?
- Was the greeting clear and easy to understand?
- Did the staff member give you their name and ask for yours?
- Were you put on hold and, if so, for how long?
- Were you asked if you needed anything else before the call was ended?

Once these activities were completed, the mystery shopper would compile a report detailing their experiences and this would be submitted to the bank manager. The name of any staff members who interacted with the mystery shopper would be included in the reports. Based on the reports, each branch was scored out of 100 and the scores were shared across all branches around Australia.

For some staff this process was very motivational because they wanted to achieve the highest score – not only for themselves but also for their branch. For other staff, this process created stress. The idea of publicly letting the branch down was too much and, at the thought of being 'mystery shopped', once happy and fabulous customer service providers became nervous and paranoid.

Mystery shopping today

Many businesses still use the mystery shopping process to gain information about their products and processes, as well as the people skills of their staff. Some also use the process as a way to 'keep staff on their toes'.

However, what is now very common is for businesses to seek the same information not from a 'secret shopper' but from their actual customers. Businesses are investing in customer service insights programs, for example, which can involve many different platforms that are used to seek feedback from their potential or existing customers. These programs are all about assessing the experience that the customer had with a business.

Some examples of customer insights programs include:

- direct telephone calls
- emailed surveys
- paper surveys given to customers
- review and star rating options on the internet
- text messages asking for a 1 to 5 rating of recent experiences.

As a customer, you have probably already completed one or more of the items from the preceding list. If you use eBay, for example, you may have noticed the stars beside the sellers' names. These stars indicate how their customers rate the sellers for their service and the products that they provide. If you've been on a holiday or stayed in a hotel, you may have been asked to complete a survey about your stay. Perhaps you bought some books or paid a bill online and were asked to rate the experience. These are all forms of customer insights programs that are utilised by a business. They gather the same information as a mystery shopper would but the information is now coming from actual or potential customers.

Customer service providers across the world are being 'mystery shopped' every day.

Why are businesses doing this?

Imagine you own your own business. Now ask yourself:

- Would you want to know if staff were ignoring your customers?
- Would you want to know if your customers didn't like your products or services?
- Would you want to know what your customers liked about your business?
- Would you want to know what more you could do to keep your customers coming back?

Mystery shopping and customer service insights programs are used to find out how customers are thinking and feeling about the business. Instead of feeling stressed about these programs, or worried you might let yourself or your company down, understand that the information can be used to make product and process improvements and also be a great help to the employees. Customer insights can confirm if staff would benefit from product, process or people skills training, and can also identify if staff would be better suited to different areas of the business. Customer feedback is essential for a business.

> The more information you and the business you work for have about your customers' needs, likes and wants, the better equipped you are to keep your customers happy.

What to do if you get a bad review

I've certainly had this happen to me. Yes, even this customer service professional has had that uncomfortable experience of not being able to please, let alone delight, a customer, and the customer has decided my boss needed to know about it. Part of being a customer service professional is being realistic and open to feedback – the good and the not so good.

No matter how much you know, how hard you try and how good your intentions are, you can't please all the customers, all of the time. Give yourself a break and remember that when you choose to interact with every customer like a customer service professional, the good feedback will far outweigh the bad.

Take negative feedback on board and if you identify something you could improve on, feel confident that you will do better next time. Try not to let one bad review cause you to doubt your abilities. Just like you, customers can have bad moments or bad days. Their interaction with you could have been when they were feeling less than positive and perhaps they judged you a little harshly.

Mystery shoppers action

Next time you go shopping where you need to interact with a customer service provider, turn on your inner mystery shopper to assess these five things:

1. How long before a staff member acknowledged you with a genuine smile?
2. When you asked for help to find something, what was the body language and tone of voice of the staff member like?
3. When paying for your purchase, did the staff member engage genuinely with you?
4. Would you recommend this business to friends or family? Why or why not?
5. What could staff have been done to improve your experience with this business?

N

IS FOR NON-NEGOTIABLE

Becoming a customer service
professional is as much about what
you do, as what you don't do.

CATE SCHRECK (YES, THAT'S ME!)

Think of a time when you were really annoyed by a customer service person you interacted with. What was it in particular that they did or said that made you annoyed? Take a moment to write down or think of the words that explain exactly what they did that made you feel that way.

Over the many years of my career and after asking that question to attendees at my training, I have identified the ten most common examples of bad customer service. These are almost guaranteed to make your customers want to complain – and essentially make your job harder.

Perhaps the reason for your own annoying experience is featured on my list.

The good news is that once you are aware of these top ten, all you have to do is make a conscious effort to never do them in your role as a customer service professional. These can become your non-negotiables.

How to annoy your customers

The ten things guaranteed to annoy customers are as follows:

1. *No greeting.* Not greeting your customers is like letting strangers walk into your home without acknowledging them. You don't have to engage in a lengthy conversation but if a customer can see you, you should let them know you've also seen them. Depending on your role, consider what you can do to avoid customers wondering if you know they exist. For example, you could:

    *   give them immediate eye contact and a genuine smile
    *   greet them using their name or 'Sir' or 'Madam'
    *   offer them your handshake
    *   offer to store their coat or umbrella (or similar)
    *   show them to a comfortable waiting area or table
    *   offer them a beverage
    *   provide them with access to device chargers, a laptop or a telephone, as required.

2. *Not being able to find staff:* Most customers become very annoyed very quickly if they have to go looking for staff to answer a question, help them find what they want or to process their purchases. This problem needs to be addressed as a team but, for

you as an individual, if your role is to be available to customers, be available. Don't have your back turned to the entrance or become so engrossed on other parts of your job that you forget to keep an eye out for customers who need your help. Customer service professionals don't hide. They stay in clear view of the customers and they communicate with other team members to take over if they have to complete tasks that will take them out of view.

3. *Having to repeat a request or information:* When a co-worker refers a customer to you, make a habit of asking your co-worker exactly what the customer has already told them – even if this is just the customer's name. This requires everyone in your team to seek to avoid needing to ask a customer to repeat information, and is especially vital when taking telephone messages. Take notes of the key words or issues the customer has stated so you can not only confirm you heard correctly but also pass this information on. The next person should then greet the customer and again, repeat to the customer what they already know.

4. *Experiencing fake interactions:* Your customers know when you are not genuinely interested in them. Make sure your body language, tone of voice and words are all giving the same message – 'I value you and I am here to help you.' Remember your body language and your tone of voice tells a customer how you really feel. Check in with yourself – what's going on that you have to fake it? If you need a break or need to move into a more positive mindset, do what you have to do to shift your attitude to that of a customer service professional.

5. *Hearing private conversations between staff:* It doesn't matter if you are talking about a social topic or a work topic, when a customer is within eye sight or earshot, give them your full attention. If your co-worker discussion is relevant to work and must be completed, still stop talking and acknowledge your customer and advise that you will be with them shortly, or find another staff member to help them. Remember – customers are paying your wage, so treat them accordingly.

6. *Putting up with poor product and process knowledge:* Most customers are more than happy for you to admit that you are new or don't have all the information they need – as long as you can confidently refer them to another staff member or take the steps to get the information to them in an agreed time frame. On the other hand, most customers become very annoyed when employees who have poor product or process knowledge make no effort to find the right answers, refer them to the wrong person or try to 'fake' their way through in the hope that the customer won't work out that they have little or no clue. Remember – customers today routinely do their research before they even speak to a customer service person, so they will probably know enough to know you are faking it.

7. *Not feeling a sense of importance:* Learn to read the level of importance your customer places on their interaction with you and seek to confirm to them you place the same level of importance on the issue. This is not about speed, this is about respect. Customers who are in a state of distress or uncertainty feel even greater levels of anxiety if the customer service provider shows no understanding of their state of mind. Use eye contact

and nodding to show you are listening, and include empathy statements to confirm you are aware of their level of importance. For example:

- 'I can see you are concerned about this and I am here to help.'
- 'Thank you for telling me; I have taken notes and will process the request right away.'

After listening to the customer and promising to respond, stand tall, walk with purpose and avoid being interrupted. You don't need to run, but if you slouch off and stop to chat to others along the way, your customer will doubt your sincerity.

8. *Staff being too pushy:* Although some customers need help to make decisions, no-one likes to feel that they are being rushed. When we rush a customer, they may make a purchase but they often leave the business feeling annoyed and will either return the product or they won't return to the business. Some evidence supports the idea that suggestive selling works (like the classic, 'Would you like fries with that?) and evidence also shows that customers who touch or feel a product are one step closer to buying. Pushy is not about using sales tactics or noticing these details – pushy is when you disregard a customer's obvious lack of interest or even more obvious 'no'.

9. *Having to do their own follow-up:* Ever had a customer service person tell you they would call you back, and they never did? Ever ordered a product and gone to pick it up on the advised date and it wasn't ready? Drives you crazy, doesn't it?! When circumstances related to a customer's purchase or a promise you have made change, you must keep the customer involved and updated on these changes or on progress. Yes, this requires

everyone in the workplace to communicate progress so that at least one person can advise the customer of any updates. Text messages are a great way today to keep customers informed of progress but if the progress includes delays or price changes, ring the customer so you can further explain the reasons.

10. *Not taking details correctly:* This is a big pet hate of mine but it also is for most customers. You can imagine how many times both my first and last name (Cate Schreck) are spelled incorrectly, but it's not just names that can be recorded incorrectly, and the things that are often recorded incorrectly are the simple things, such as addresses, dates, times, costs and measurements. (This is covered further in the 'Q is for Quality and Quantity' chapter.) Always repeat details back to a customer at least once.

Case study of bad – and good – customer service

I recently went into a department store seeking to purchase some kitchenware. As I entered the store I was greeted with, well, nothing. I made eye contact with a sales person but she didn't smile or say anything. Indeed, she appeared to not even register I was there. I wandered around and eventually found something I wanted to purchase. I walked up to the sales counter – and no-one was there. I wandered around some more and found another staff member and asked if he could process my transaction. He sighed and said, very reluctantly, 'Yes, but this isn't my department. Mary should be here.' I put the item down on the counter, advised him I had changed my mind and I left the department store.

I then went into another shop and started browsing. From somewhere behind a counter I heard a bright, friendly voice say, 'Hi there, I won't be long but yell out if you need any help.' I said I was fine browsing and she left me alone. As soon as she saw me approach the counter with my items, she immediately stopped what she was doing and came over to process the transaction. When she processed my transaction with my credit card, she saw my name and commented on the spelling. (As you can imagine, not only does the spelling of my name cause problems, but my surname – Schreck – also causes all manner of fun conversations.) We shared a giggle about the *Shrek* movies and, while she was wrapping my parcel, she welcomed another customer into the store with eye contact and a smile. My purchase was quite heavy so she asked how far I had to walk and offered to double bag the item for extra support. After all this great service, where do you think I'll go next time I need kitchenware? Oh, and did I mention that I paid $15 more for the item?

It's fair to say that I may just be every customer service provider's worst nightmare, because I do set the bar high when it comes to the level of service I expect. But I can tell you, it's a bar that everyone can reach and it only takes a second. Customers want the same thing from their customer service providers today – attention and a polite and friendly smile.

> **No customer likes to be ignored and no customer complains about a friendly smile.**

Understanding the consequences of bad customer service

Think of the last time you had a negative experience with a business. Do you remember the name of the customer service person or do you remember the name of the business? Customers often hang on to their examples of a bad customer service experience and share them over and over again, even years later. What they tend to forget is the name of the person who served them. What they always remember is the name of the business.

Don't think that since your name is forgotten you get off easily. I'm sure you can think of businesses that have a bad reputation for customer service. Everyone who works in those businesses is now considered as being bad at customer service. Even though those businesses will have customer service professionals working for them, it's the untrained customer service people who are having a negative effect on the reputation of everyone in the team and the reputation of the business as a whole.

I mention in the 'H is for Handling Complaints' chapter a statistic from the 1980s that 'Unhappy customers will tell 8 to 16 people if they have a bad experience with a business'. I also ask you in that chapter to imagine the reach that unhappy customers have today with the social media avenues they have access to. A customer's level of satisfaction is paramount for a business to succeed. Businesses today collate and review customer feedback (the good, the bad and the ugly) because it's the customers who determine where they will spend their money – which, ultimately, creates your wage.

Customer service professionals know this and they are ready to fix, repair, listen to and respect the needs of the unhappy customer, and they do it so well that the unhappy customer will then tell their friends and family about the amazing service – and the customer service professional gets the credit for it.

Understanding the value of complaints and becoming confident in handling those difficult interactions will give you great personal and career satisfaction – which, in turn, means less stress.

Non-negotiable action

1. Review the top ten list of things almost guaranteed to make your customers want to complain, and share it with your team.

2. Place a copy of the list where you can refer to it often – just make sure it's out of your customers' eyesight.

O

IS FOR OVER AND ABOVE

A customer is the most important visitor on our premises.
He is not dependent on us. We are dependent on him.
He is not an interruption in our work. He is the purpose of it.
He is not an outsider in our business. He is part of it.
We are not doing him a favour by serving him.
He is doing us a favour by giving us an opportunity to do so.

BASED ON PRINCIPLES ORIGINALLY OUTLINED
BY KENNETH B ELLIOTT IN 1941

Recently I visited my hairdressers and I just love going there – and my enjoyment is not about what they do to my hair. It's based on how everyone in the team treats me. The experience starts with the genuine smiles as soon as I walk in the door, and then continues as they use my name and immediately offer me coffee, tea or water (and the beverage of my choice always comes with a yummy shortbread on the side).

Whenever I ring the salon, I get the same positive and friendly greeting and the same level of service. They have always done this. They have never taken it for granted that I will come back. They make me feel like I matter, like I am doing them a favour by being their customer.

What this team does is provide me with a level of service that is over and above my expectation, and they have done this consistently for more than six years.

And the reason this level of service is so vital is because they have people who deliver their services – and people make mistakes. Based on the service I receive, however, I would still return to them if they made a few mistakes.

I describe this type of customer service as putting credits into a customer's 'bank of service excellence'. My hairdressers have put so many credits in the bank of service excellence that I would forgive them some mistakes. In my eyes, they are in credit and, as long as they stay in credit, I'll stay as their customer. And I'll keep referring my friends and family to them. Because of their current service, they don't have to rely heavily on marketing and other tactics to get new customers; their service is so good, their existing customers send new customers to them.

> **The cheapest and most effective form of marketing is excellent service.**

To give ourselves room for the unforeseen, every person in the business who interacts with external customers should take every opportunity to exceed that customer's expectations. Again, this helps put credit into the customer's bank of service excellence.

The bank of service excellence

Customers love it when a customer service person gives them more than they expected – and I'm not talking about the product or service they were buying. I'm referring to the experience they had while they interacted with the business. When a customer interacts with a business, they will – consciously or subconsciously – calculate the number of positive experiences they have with the business. The more positive experiences they have, the less chance they will leave or take their money elsewhere if things go wrong.

When the positive experiences outweigh the negative and something unforeseen happens, customers have enough evidence of the business being excellent that most customers (no, not all) will tolerate mistakes. A mistake is a withdrawal from the bank of service excellence but if the business has put enough positive credits in the bank, the withdrawal will still leave the customer with enough credits to keep coming back.

Essentially it's about the feeling that the customer is left with after every interaction with the business. This process requires great teamwork as everyone a customer interacts with should be aiming to put credits in the bank of service excellence.

Never over-promise and underdeliver

Ever had a customer service person tell you they would have something ready by a certain date or time, and then they didn't? Perhaps you were expecting a call back or a home visit and they didn't achieve that promise. This type of error can take many credits out the bank of service excellence.

> **When we make a customer a promise, it is the most important thing you have said to them.**

Watching what you promise to customers is particularly important for customer service providers in a new role. While you are learning, it can be tempting to avoid telling customers you don't know or need help because you fear them getting upset or becoming annoyed with you. Trust me when I say that guessing or making things up is not the way to go and it will make things worse in the long run. One of the best ways to learn is to jump right in and start interacting with customers; just do it like a customer service professional.

In the 'C is for Communication' chapter, I emphasise that it's not what you say but how you say it. New customer service providers can avoid the trap of over-promising and underdelivering by saying something like the following statements and remembering to use a polite and friendly tone and give your customer a sense of confidence with eye contact and a smile. If in any doubt, use something similar to these statements:

- 'I've just started working here so I am going to get someone who can answer this for you.'
- 'I'm new to this business and want to make sure you get the right answer, I'll just speak to my …'
- 'I'm not 100 per cent sure of that because I am new to this team. Let me just check with my …'

Trying to meet customers' expectations can be tempting, but sometimes what a customer's wants and what you can do are two different things.

How your pay and your service are linked

In America, hospitality or service staff receive a base wage and rely on monetary tips to increase their earnings. The tips are directly related to the customer's perception of the level of service they received from the staff.

Oh dear, imagine that. What if your customers decided how much wage you would get based solely on your customer service skills? Australian customers don't follow the tipping system as strictly, but I want you to start considering every single customer as if they are paying your wage – because they are.

That's right. Your external customers are paying your wage.

It's like this:

- Businesses exist to meet the demand for their products and/or services.
- Without external customers using or buying the products or services, the business receives no money.
- No money means the business can't pay wages.
- No wages means no you.

When you don't provide a service that leaves your customers feeling respected and valued, they will easily be swayed to spend their money (your wage) elsewhere. They may take their money (your wage) to a competitor, who may eventually take all of your customers, and then your business is out of customers and, well, you are out of a job.

'But,' I hear you say, 'our customers don't have a choice because they can only get the services or products we offer from us.' Well, consider this: customers who have no choice but to do business with you will not willingly give you their money (your wage). Your days will be spent dealing with grumpy customers, handling complaints and generally feeling unsatisfied at work.

Oh, and before you know it, they will also tell everyone else who must do business with you about your poor service, and these potential customers won't want to do business with you even before they have met you. Phew ... exhausting, isn't it.

Understanding over-servicing

As opposed to over-promising and underdelivering, over-servicing is essentially doing more than the customer expected but not adding any real value to the customer. It's like taking your customer's food order and then going away, printing it up on nice paper and bringing it back to them to keep so they can remember what they ordered. It's a nice gesture and surely shows you care about them but it's not necessary and will ultimately take you away from doing other more important tasks – like ensuring their food gets to their table as soon as it's ready and serving other customers.

Okay, so that may seem like an extreme example but my point is this: customer service professionals, although always seeking ways to exceed customers' expectations, don't get carried away with adding extra one-off things.

Over-servicing can also be annoying to customers. Imagine going into a shop and having the shop assistant follow you around, offer to hold your items, put your rubbish in the bin and tell you all about the prices as you wander. Customer service professionals read what a customer wants via their body language and tone of voice and they aim to make the shopping experience as pleasant as possible – and stalking is usually a no-no.

Over-servicing potentially comes with one other problem. If you go out of your way to give a customer an absolutely amazing experience by doing one-off wonderful things, they may leave singing your praises, but you have now set a very high bar for yourself and for every other customer service provider in your business. You and all other service providers now have to provide the same level of service the next time the customer arrives.

> **Stick to a level of service that everyone on the team can achieve.**

Over and above action

Develop a list of things that would potentially exceed your customer's expectations and that your workplace may be able to provide or that everyone in your team can do. For example:

1. have a water cooler accessible in the customer area
2. have competitions that your customers can be a part of
3. acknowledge customer birthdays and special events – and be genuine when you do so
4. invite customers to join your team in charity events
5. ask your customers what you could do to improve your service – simple but effective
6. provide tissues in the customer area
7. have a children's play area with books, toys and so on
8. have a daily roster for staff to monitor the tidiness of the customer area
9. run free information sessions for the customers to learn about your business
10. have live plants in the customer area.

P

IS FOR PRESENTATION

*Happiness is reaching the bottom
of the ironing basket.*

EVERY PERSON WHO HATES IRONING (INCLUDING ME)

Think for a minute about how much attention you pay to your presentation in one or all of the following scenarios:

- job interview
- first date
- meeting your partner's parents or loved ones
- first day in a new job
- meeting someone you admire.

All of the preceding situations usually have us wanting to make good first impressions, and we know that people will form an opinion on not only what we say, but also how we dress and how we behave. As is commonly said, you only get one chance to make a good first impression, but customer service professionals pay attention to how they look and how they behave every day, because they know that every interaction with a customer matters – not just the first one.

Countless studies show that people will form their impression of you within the first eight seconds. But it's no coincidence that lawyers spend an inordinate amount of time crafting a powerful and persuasive closing statement at the end of the trial – because they know it can have an extremely influential effect on the jury.

So, with this in mind, if you want to be a customer service professional, don't put all your energy into making a great first impression and forget about anything else. The last impression you leave a customer with will be the one they remember most.

Caring about what you wear

Customer service employees can commonly fall into bad habits when it comes to their presentation. During my time as a customer service manager and also when working to help job seekers gain employment, I had to have conversations with people about inappropriate clothing choices and grooming shortfalls.

Professional presentation doesn't mean expensive clothing. Fantastic second-hand clothing outlets can provide a huge range of professional clothing. You can spend as little as $1 for a black jacket or you can spend $1,000 – both jackets will be considered professional if they are in good condition, clean and fit you well.

Professional presentation goes beyond the right jacket, however. The following list outlines the seven most common presentation issues I have had to address with staff and job seekers. As you look through this list, also keep in mind that different businesses will have different presentation standards so it's up to you to find out what they are and abide by them. As a start, definitely avoid the following:

1. underwear showing – including bra straps, G-strings and/or briefs
2. unironed, stained or smelly clothing
3. scuffed or worn-out footwear
4. sweat-stained shirts – particularly the underarms
5. cuffs and hems coming undone
6. body odour – not the nice smells
7. excessive use of fragrances – cologne or perfume.

> The type of business you work for will determine what clothing is acceptable. If in doubt, find out what your employer expects.

I was always uncomfortable having to have conversations with employees and job seekers about the issues in the preceding list, but most times the individual, although embarrassed, appreciated that I'd had the conversation with them in private and allowed them the opportunity to provide reasons, apologise and seek ways to improve.

You may think some of the things on the preceding list are overly judgemental. Many workplaces today allow their employees to wear what they find comfortable, and that allows employees to show their creativity or uniqueness. Again, expectations depend on what type of business you work for. If you work in a clothing store that sells tracksuits or jeans, wearing these kinds of products may not only be acceptable but also encouraged by the workplace. If you work in a funeral parlour, however, the clothing standard may be more formal, such as a suit.

Overall, customer service professionals understand that a workplace has hygiene and clothing standards. These standards may not be what you agree with. I personally *hate* ironing. I am more than happy to wear unironed clothes in my private time but I know that if I interact with customers and my clothes are unironed, it sends a message that I don't care much about my presentation. This can leave my customers concerned that my attention to detail may lack in other areas too – like designing and delivering their customer service training programs.

> How you look and how you act gives customers an insight into how good you are at your job.

Presentation of your work area

If you have your own desk or work area, how you present that area provides an insight into how organised you are. You may like to work in what is often referred to as 'organised chaos' but if your workspace can be viewed by external customers, it's time to tidy up. Working in organised chaos in your private life may be perfectly okay, but at work, customers like to do business with people who are organised and a messy work area will be perceived as disorganised.

> An untidy work area can be evidence of low or no organisational skills.

Depending on the amount of your 'organised chaos', you may need to spend a bit of time getting yourself in order. Once you've made the effort to get organised, make the most of it by spending just five minutes at the end of every day getting it back to that state. You can go home and mess up your place as much as you want – unless you share with others, then you might have a different set of rules to abide by. Living alone does have its benefits.

Your after-hours presentation

Does your presentation still matter after hours? Yes, but let me explain …

Imagine you work as a customer service provider for a bakery called Bread Heaven and one of the ovens has stopped working. The owner is fully aware of this but, unfortunately, there is a three-week delay on getting it fixed. One oven out of order means no dinner rolls and this causes complaints from customers – and you have to handle the complaints.

You get through the first week of 'dinner roll riots' and one day on your way home from work, you stop off at the supermarket to buy your groceries. While you are walking the aisles, an older gentleman comes up to you and asks if you could pass him something off a top shelf. You smile and happily pass him the product. The nice older gentleman says thank you and laughingly suggests that 'You could get a job here'. You say in a sarcastic tone, 'I would if I could because at least the customers are nice here and the machines work.'

Now here's the bad news. That lovely gentleman notices the logo on your shirt so he knows where you work – and he is a regular customer of Bread Heaven. You have just given the impression that Bread Heaven uses faulty machinery and they have rude customers. That lovely gentleman plays bowls every weekend with 50 other people who also like to get their bread from Bread Heaven. Your trivial, after-hours comment has serious repercussions that may affect your wage – remember, it's your customers who pay your wage.

Bread Heaven is the name of a business but when *you* are interacting with people, *you* are Bread Heaven, even when you are off the clock. Even if the nice gentleman remains a customer, your opinion has sowed a seed of doubt in his mind and when a customer suspects a business (*you*) is losing interest in them, they will start to lose interest too, and before long, your wage may be going to another business.

Every business has 'breakdowns' of some kind and will not be able to meet all of your needs, all of the time. Remember the big picture. The repair of an oven – although vital in your role – can be further down the list of priorities for the business. Customer service professionals respect this and they always speak highly of the business in the public eye. (This doesn't mean you can never complain or vent when you have frustrations – see 'V is for Venting' for more on this.)

> **While you are wearing the uniform of the business, you are the business.**

Presenting yourself via Social Media

Have you ever asked yourself one (or more) of the following:

- Can I rant about my workplace to my friends on social media?
- Is it okay to complain about a customer on social media if I don't use their name?
- Surely an employer can't control my after-hour social media fun?

Most employers today will have set policies on the use of social media and the expectations of you while you are their employee. In some instances, employees have lost their jobs for ignoring or disobeying these rules. If in doubt, find out what your employer's expectations are.

Let's look at one example of why social media rules exist. Say an employee of a plumbing business took a photo of himself on his lunch break, sitting in front of his employer's truck while he was having a smoke. He posted this on his Facebook page with the comment: 'Great day for chilling out'. Seems harmless enough right? Wrong.

What he didn't know was that as a natural course of business, his employer uses programs to search the internet for signs of his business name. (Many employers do this to keep informed of how the business is being represented online.) This picture was reported as putting the company in a negative light and so the employee was asked to take the photo and the comment down.

The employee become enraged at the request to remove what he thought was just a harmless photo. What he didn't understand and appreciate was that the photo was also shared across other social media platforms by unhappy customers to prove that the company had lazy employees. The employee had to undertake training to help him gain a better understanding of how and why his social media activities could have an impact on his employment. This didn't stop him from continuing to post similar photos, however, and he eventually lost his job.

Did you know that it's also not uncommon for employers to search social media platforms to determine if job candidates would suit the role they are applying for? They sure do. Like it or not, you are who Google says you are, so have fun with social media but know the rules in relation to both your workplace and how you may present yourself to future employers.

If in doubt, find out.

Presentation action

Not sure if your presentation could do with a bit of help? Worried that your perfume or body odour is causing others to back away from you?

Ask a trusted friend to give you honest feedback or enlist the services of a professional. Many style and image consultants are available to help you present professionally, and some of these are relatively inexpensive. If money is an issue, consider options such as Lifeline Shops, where you can find great quality clothing while also helping to fund the Lifeline Hotline, and services such as Fitted for Work (www.fittedforwork.org) and Wear for Success (www.wearforsuccess.org.au). These services can not only provide clothes but also help with work and presentation skills.

Q

IS FOR QUALITY AND QUANTITY

*People forget how fast
you did a job – but they remember
how well you did it.*

HOWARD NEWTON

Consider this: you are really thirsty. It's a very hot day and you know two businesses nearby can sell you a drink of water.

Say you walk in the door of business number one and are asked to take a seat at a table with a beautiful view and flowers on the table. Lovely music is playing and the smell of freshly baked biscuits wafts past your nose. A waiter comes over, introduces himself and welcomes you with a friendly smile. He asks for your name and tells you a story about the water they sell. He tells you how the water was sourced, filtered and transported on the backs of donkeys through rough terrain. He tells you about the specially designed refrigeration trucks that deliver the water to the business and how it is stored on site, laying undisturbed on beds of cotton in recycled bottles until a customer purchases it. The waiter then pours the water for you and, while you are quenching your thirst, he tells you about the special biscuits you can also purchase.

Alternatively, you can go to business number two, a café, open a fridge door, get a bottle of water and take it to the counter, pay for it and drink it as you leave. No story, no table cloth and no names exchanged – and no offer of biscuits.

Business number one is all about quality service. The product is basically the same as that provided in option two but, as you access the product, the first business has chosen to add a quality level of customer service.

Business number two is all about a quantity level of service – that is, serve as many customers as possible.

Both options achieve the same outcome and neither is wrong – the customer makes a decision based on their own needs. Maybe you just want to get your water, without the long back story. But still, option two could have been better, much better.

Quality versus quantity service

A quality business is designed to provide an experience through the products or services it provides. The approach here is all about giving the customer a quality experience while they are purchasing or accessing the products or services on offer. A fine dining restaurant, where the aim is to give customers high-quality food and a high-quality experience while they are dining, is an example of quality service. Attention will be paid to the table setting, the noise level of the surrounds, the decor, the menu design and the soft and hard skills of the staff. Of course, this type of service generally comes with a higher price tag.

A quantity business is designed to provide products and services to customers in the most efficient way possible. Supermarkets are a great example of a quantity service. The products are all out on display for the customer to help themselves, and they can choose to either line up for a checkout operator to process the transactions or they can do it themselves in the self-service payment area. Supermarket customers can choose to get in, get what they need, pay and leave – all without interacting with a service provider. Supermarkets don't require their staff to get to know the customer's name, tell them about the products or do anything more than get them in and get them out. It's what the customers want – fast access to the products and a fast exit from the business.

The problem with the quantity service process is that when we focus on doing things quickly, we can leave the customers feeling rushed and ignored. Customer service staff can inadvertently get caught up in quantity mode and this can make the customer feel as if they are an annoyance or even an interruption. Ultimately, the customer service provider and the business can be considered as rude and uncaring.

Although your customers may be time-poor or choosing to do business with you because of your 'help yourself' options, this doesn't mean they want to be ignored totally.

> The quality part of customer service is related to your soft skills. The quantity part of customer service is related to your hard skills.

Using your soft and hard skills together

In the 'K is for Knowledge' chapter, I go into some detail on hard and soft skills. Here's a quick rundown on how these skills relate to quality or quantity style of service:

- *Soft skills = quality:* Soft skills such as smiling, making eye contact, listening, being aware of your own mood, speaking professionally to co-workers, stopping co-worker conversations if a customer requires help, using customers' names when possible, greeting customers, offering help and thanking customers are all required for quality service styles.
- *Hard skills = quantity:* Tangible hard skills such as taking orders efficiently, processing purchases, using equipment, typing, stocking shelves, driving a fork lift and entering data are more the focus for quantity service styles.

You can increase the speed of your hard skills by practising. Think of it like this: when you get a new mobile phone, you have to look at the screen to do everything. But after a while you're able to complete all the necessary tasks pretty much blindfolded. Using a mobile phone is a hard skill – just like using a cash register, scanning, ordering or typing into a database. Practise will increase your speed and more practise will improve your efficiency.

Customer service professionals can perform the hard skills of their role with speed and efficiency, which allows them to then concentrate on their soft skills.

> Customers of any business remember how you made them feel.

Case study of quantity and quality

When I was working in the bank, peak periods would require us to move into a quantity service mode. Some customers would come into the branch to use the self-serve options and others would have to join the queue to interact with our staff. Customers hate queues. The quicker we could process transactions and get them on their way, the happier they were. We still smiled, we still used their names but we didn't seek to engage a customer for a lengthy conversation – which we would normally do to help build rapport and offer new products. Customers who were using the self-service options still liked to know a staff member was on hand if they had any questions, so we always had someone within eye and earshot of those customers too.

Even outside of peak periods, customer service professionals use their detective skills to assess the body language and tone of voice of their customers to determine if they are time-poor. Customers who are time-poor value customer service providers who act with a sense of urgency too. The skill is in getting everything done efficiently while also providing a quality level of service.

Whether you choose to provide a quality service when you are in a quantity business or peak period of your quality business all comes down to your WIIFM (What's In It For Me? – see the 'I is for Internal Motivation' chapter).

> Quality service takes no more time – it simply takes more focus.

Quality and quantity action

Next time you go to a quantity business such as a fast-food takeaway business, supermarket or petrol station, assess whether the service person is only focused on processing the transaction/s (quantity service) or is choosing to also provide a quality service like a customer service professional. Consider the following:

- Did they give you a genuine smile and eye contact?
- Did they talk to you?
- What did their tone of voice and body language tell you about how they felt?
- Did any other staff acknowledge you?

If you think it really doesn't matter consider this: I have known many business owners or managers to approach customer service professionals who work in quantity businesses and offer them jobs, based purely on their ability to multi-task their hard and soft skills. Customer service professionals are highly sought after and you never know who's watching you.

R

IS FOR REALITY CHECK

If it is to be it is up to me.

WILLIAM H JOHNSON

If you're seeking or just started in a customer service role, this chapter will give you an insight into what could happen in your future. If you've been providing customer service for years, this chapter is a chance for you to take a step back and re-assess your perception of the job.

Perhaps at some point you've found yourself mumbling these words – or something like them:

- 'I could get so much more done if the customers would stop interrupting me.'
- 'I'm so sick of having to repeat the same thing to different people all day, every day.'

- 'I've got so many things to do that serving customers is just wasting my time.'

When I hear these or similar statements from customer service providers today, it tells me they need a reality check. They've lost sight of the value they have in the workplace and the power they have to have a positive impact on the lives of others.

Sometimes the reason for the provider's attitude is because they would be better placed in a different role. I ask them to consider these questions:

- Would you prefer a role that has little or no interaction with external customers?
- When you meet a stranger for the first time, do you smile warmly and welcome the chance to engage with someone new or do you prefer to remain a little reserved until you have determined if they are friend or foe?

Some people find it much easier to only interact with internal customers, because of reasons like the following:

- You can spend more time with them.
- You can speak the language of the workplace with them (using jargon and acronyms, for example).
- You can build not only strong workplace relationships but also great friendships.
- You can be honest with them about how you are feeling.
- You can go to them for help.

External customers are equivalent to strangers. On first meeting, you don't know anything about them – they could be easy to communicate with or difficult; they may ask you something you don't have the answer to; or they may want to complain and you're going to be put under pressure. Maybe they will be a new friend – but you don't know.

> 💡 **The idea of interacting with a stranger makes some people feel uncomfortable.**

Nothing is wrong with admitting that interacting with strangers doesn't excite you, and that you feel it puts a bit of pressure on you. Admitting this doesn't mean you can't provide excellent service, but you may find doing so takes more effort. Please, make the effort because your external customers will be able to tell if you don't genuinely want to interact with them.

Let me give you an example. I recently went to a coffee shop to meet up with a business colleague. The outside of the coffee shop was very inviting and inside the fit-out was modern, the chairs were comfortable and the food on display looked very tasty. I stood at the counter and waited for someone to serve me. After about 20 seconds, a man came up to stand beside me and asked what I would like. I assumed he worked there so I ordered my coffee, sat down and waited for my colleague. The man wandered off out of sight. With no signs of my coffee being made, I started to wonder if he did work there – maybe he just liked asking people what they would like?

My colleague arrived five minutes later and I was still without my coffee. I went back to the counter and, again, after about 20 seconds the same man appeared, this time on the other side of the counter. I repeated my order and also ordered my colleagues' drink. The man looked at me as if he had never seen me before, but this time he wrote down the order and then passed it to his co-worker. The co-worker didn't say anything – they didn't even look at each other – and they both wandered off in different directions.

Now, I know I have high expectations of customer service providers but this was surely never going to meet anyone's expectations. So, what was the problem? Why were these people roaming around like zombies? Of course, 100 different things could have fuelled such unprofessional behaviour, but if these people genuinely liked interacting with external customers, the other things wouldn't matter. They would choose a professional attitude and not let a customer know how they feel.

A reality check if external customers have become hard work

As I've outlined in other chapters, our body language and tone of voice tells people how we feel and what our attitude is, so if you're not enjoying your job or find interacting with external customers hard work, maybe it's time for your reality check. The following sections outline the most common questions or concerns presented to me when I am coaching customer service providers. They also provide some help with these common problems.

Am I part of the problem?

If dealing with customers all day every day leaves you exhausted or causes you anxiety, remember that customers will read this in your body language and tone of voice, thus increasing the chances of a customer complaining about your poor service.

If you no longer – or never did – enjoy meeting, greeting and serving external customers you can still be a customer service professional – behind the scenes. Internal customer service is just as vital as external customer service because everyone in the business has a responsibility to provide great service to each other. You might just be better suited to working on your internal customer relationships and aiming to become an internal customer service professional.

Many roles in a business have little or no external customer interaction – for example:

- audit or quality assurance
- bookkeeping/accounting
- cleaning/night fill/merchandising
- data entry/design/development
- manufacturing – process and production
- project management
- research and data analysis
- warehousing and storage.

Have I become complacent?

According to the Oxford Dictionary, complacent means 'Showing smug or uncritical satisfaction with oneself or one's achievements'. If you've been in the same customer service role for a few or many years, now is the time to self-assess that you haven't started to become complacent. Complacency as a customer service person shows up in the little things. We may or may not realise it but we can get lazy or think that we don't have to pay as much attention to all our service skills as we did when we first started the job. We may have lost sight of the bigger picture and the value of our role.

The longer the customer has been with the business, the more they have examples of your great service. Don't let them down or risk them leaving by thinking they no longer require you to be excellent. Don't take your customers for granted.

> It's your customers who determine if you are an excellent service provider – not you.

Don't be too hard on yourself if complacency has taken hold – it's not unusual and you can fix it.

Here is a list of the basics of customer service for you to review and put back into your service provision:

- acknowledge or greet customers instantly
- use a customer's name
- double-check the spelling of customers' names
- advise how long customers will have to wait and keep them up to date with any delays or changes
- ask open questions to confirm their needs
- say please and thank you
- slow down – rushing can come across as panicking.

> Customer service professionals benefit from an annual service excellence check-up.

I'm sick of dealing with difficult customers

Over time, you may have had one too many grumpy, difficult or rude customer interactions, and this may have left you feeling like a 'punching bag'. Maybe the idea of quitting has been invading your thoughts. Maybe you're losing your ability to control your emotions at work. Before you decide to chuck everything in and quit, however, these five reality checks might help change your perspective:

1. Are you clear on what you dislike about your job or do you just need a break?
2. When did you last have at least two weeks away from work? If it's more than 12 months ago, you're overdue.
3. Customer service providers must refresh their people skills every 12 months. What have you done in the last 12 months to refresh those skills?
4. When was the last time you received positive feedback about your performance? Ask for a performance review.
5. If you must quit, remember: It's easier to get a job, when you have a job.

In relation to the final point in the preceding list, depending on your financial situation, you may be able to quit and live off your savings while you job hunt. This gives you the time and space to focus on finding a job you will enjoy and will pay the bills. If money is tight I recommend you should, if you can, stay in the job you have while you job hunt.

Needing a job quickly reduces your ability to assess job opportunities based on anything other than money. You may be very tempted to take the first job on offer – and this can be okay for the first three to six months while you settle into the new role. But often you then find yourself in the same situation of not liking the job, because you didn't fully assess the job on the internal rewards it would give you. Job hunting without a job also increases your level of anxiety and this can show in your body language and tone of voice when you attend an interview.

> Job hunting is a job in itself and is best carried out without the added pressure of the bills needing to be paid and the cupboards needing to be filled.

The following section covers this topic in more depth.

Why having a job is more important than money

If you have ever been unemployed, you will know that remaining positive and motivated about life in general can become incredibly hard. During my time as a disability employment consultant, I witnessed firsthand the stress and anxiety that being without a job can cause an individual and their family.

The absence of a job can mean:

- limited or no social life
- lower levels of confidence
- ongoing concern about your future
- restricted housing options.

When you don't have a job, you also have no answer to the question, 'What do you do?' While this might not seem as important as the issues in the preceding list, that question is how we get to know strangers, and is how we seek to understand people and learn about them. When you are job seeking, that question sucks.

If you have always had a job and you are now finding it difficult to stay focused and positive at work, don't forget that having a job, any job, is only a dream for many. I encourage you to think of your role as a customer service provider as more important than just your means for paying the bills. The world needs more people who communicate honestly and with respect. The world needs more people who understand and use emotional intelligence and who see themselves as a positive force in people's lives. The world needs more customer service professionals.

> Customer service professionals are people who consider helping people an honour. Customer service is an honourable role in every industry – be proud.

The downsides of becoming a customer service professional

Before you get too 'giddy' with your plan for customer service success, I need to bring you back to earth for just a minute. Every plan for success has to have a plan to manage the impact of the success. Every successful person knows that success does have a downside – for example:

- Successful entertainers will tell you that loss of privacy is the downside of success.
- Successful sportspeople find media commitments eat into their training time.
- Successful chefs have to keep coming up with new dishes.
- Successful writers have to learn to accept bad reviews.
- Successful doctors have to keep learning.

Customer service professionals also have to cope with some extra demands and downsides to being successful. The following outlines some of these downsides – luckily for you, I've also provided you with some tips to help you handle your success:

- Providing consistently excellent customer service can be tiring: look after yourself by knowing how to relax (refer to the 'Z is for Zen' chapter for help).
- Customers will ask for you and some will even wait to be served by you: help everyone on the team become customer service professionals so you're not always the only one in demand.
- You're going to be busy listening to compliments: improve your time management skills.
- You will be considered an expert in your industry: keep your product and service knowledge up to date.
- New staff will need your help: practise patience and remember you also had to train to be as good as you are.
- You may be given new opportunities both in and out of work: be clear on your own career and personal goals.
- Others may take advantage of you: practise saying no, and be assertive when you sense others being lazy.
- Difficult customers will still exist: never lose empathy for them.
- You may be nominated for customer service awards: gain some public speaking and/or presentation skills.
- When you are a customer, you will be disappointed when you are not served by a customer service professional: tell them about this book.

The preceding list is not definitive, but includes many downsides identified by customer service professionals.

> Customer service professionals are made, not born. Just like elite athletes, you will need to keep training to stay at the top.

Reality check action

Take the time now to do your own reality check. Reflect on how you feel about providing service to external and internal customers by creating your own pros and cons list. I've given you a couple of ideas to start you off in specific areas but cross them out if you don't agree with them.

Pros of providing service to internal customers:

- Have time to get to know each other.
- _____
- _____

Cons of providing service to internal customers:

- Can't avoid working with people you find difficult to deal with.
- _____
- _____

Pros of providing service to external customers:

- Enjoy being able to help lots of different customers.
- _____
- _____

Cons of providing service to external customers:

- Having to interact with rude or abusive customers.

- _____

- _____

When your lists are complete, have a look at everything you wrote in the cons lists and come up with ways to overcome them.

S

IS FOR SELLING

A customer doesn't care how much you know until they know how much you care.

COMMONLY ATTRIBUTED TO THEODORE ROOSEVELT

Before we really get into this chapter, ask yourself:

- Did you cringe when you saw the title of this chapter?
- Did you light up because you love selling to your customers?
- Do you think this chapter doesn't apply to you because you don't have to sell?

If you work as a customer service provider in a business that has products and services for customers to purchase, your employer may expect you to encourage your customers to buy. Some customers will come to you ready to buy and others may require some more information before they decide to buy. Either way, people like to buy from, and do business with, people they like. Your soft skills are what make you likeable – and customer service professionals have excellent soft skills and so make excellent sales people.

If you work as a customer service provider in a business that doesn't require you to sell anything specifically, you probably don't think that you require sales skills. Although you're not directly responsible for selling, however, you do represent the business and customers will also determine if they will continue to do business there based on how you interact with them.

> **You are selling something – you are selling you. And your smile is your greatest sales tool.**

Building rapport

Creating rapport with someone means connecting with them. Being able to build rapport with your customers requires you to use your soft skills, including active listening, as well as remembering your body language and tone of voice.

Often salespeople try to engage customers with small talk, which helps to build rapport, or questions that lead towards a possible sale – for example:

- 'What are you up to today?'
- 'What are your plans for the weekend?
- 'What can I help you with today?

- 'Would you like fries with that?'
- 'Can I help you find what you are looking for?'

All of the preceding options are great ways to get your customers talking, so you can then assess how they are feeling and what their attitude is. Customers will quickly let you know via their body language and tone of voice if they are keen to engage with you or want your help. The trick with building rapport is to be genuine. Use eye contact, smile and use a tone that is helpful. If you spend your day saying the same words to different customers, you might not realise how tired the words are sounding – but your customers will quickly pick up that you don't really care about them, and that you are simply saying what you have been told to say.

> People like to do business with people they like. Be genuine. Be likeable.

Change your perspective and improve your sales

It's not uncommon for the customer service providers I coach to confide in me that they don't like having to sell to their customers. They feel that selling is equal to being pushy or putting pressure on their customers, and these people generally try to avoid a role that requires them to sell because it can make them feel anxious and uncomfortable. For a while in my career, I was one of those people. What made 'selling' easier and less stressful was to remember that all I had to do was think like a customer service professional. Be a detective, actively listen and think of the potential benefits what you have to sell could create in your customer's life.

When I worked in the bank, pairing my soft skills with the potential benefits I'd identified for the customers helped me to achieve sales targets and still feel good about myself. Here are a few examples of these pairings:

- A customer mentions they are going on a holiday. This becomes an opportunity to speak about how credits cards are safer than cash.
- A customer mentions they are buying new furniture. This creates an opportunity to remind them to increase their contents insurance to include the new purchases.
- A customer has just had a child. This is an opportunity for them to consider setting up a new bank account to help save for their education.
- A customer complains about their car breaking down. This becomes an opportunity to remind them how much time and money they spend on repairs and ask them to consider a personal loan for a more reliable car.

I found selling became not only possible but also rewarding when I stopped thinking of it as 'sales' and started simply combining my soft skills with the benefits of the product in my customer's life.

Alternatively, I found it difficult to sell something I didn't think added any value to the customer's life. I didn't enjoy selling just to hit targets. This is not the case for everyone – some of you may find selling fun and are motivated by the chance of not only reaching sales targets but also exceeding them. If this is you, just be mindful that your customers still need to feel that you are helping. You could be missing out on sales because the customer suspects they are just a means for you to reach your targets.

> **Stop thinking of it as 'selling' and start thinking of it as 'helping'. And excellent service = sales.**

Your customer will lose interest in you and your business if they suspect you are losing interest in them. The easier you make it for your customers to do business with you, the more chance the customers will keep doing business with you.

Selling action

If you do have products or services to sell, write up a list of the items you need to sell and think of all the benefits this item could have for customers.

For example:

Product	Possible benefits
Mobile phone	Portable access to books, music, games, maps; instant access to family and friends
Ball	Provides fun and fitness; improves co-ordination
T-shirt	Easy to wash, no ironing, easy to store

When you are talking to customers, ask questions to determine which benefits would appeal to them most. Show that you care about your customers by listening to them and matching the benefits accordingly.

T

IS FOR TEAMWORK

*TEAM = **T**ogether **E**veryone*
***A**chieves **M**ore*

ANONYMOUS

It's time for me to confess. I used to find teamwork, hard work. Not hard in the sense of the tasks the team had to complete, but hard when it came to interacting with, well … with people. Some people could really rattle my cage, push my buttons or simply exhaust me with their chatter. And don't start me on the array of catch phrases that were trotted out to motivate and inspire me to greatness within a team. Okay, just a few then, in the spirit of venting:

- 'Get on the train to success town'
- 'There is no I in team'

- 'Surrender the ME for WE'
- 'Teamwork makes the dream work'
- 'In union there is strength'.

Don't get me wrong, for some people and some teams, the preceding statements, and the many more like them, are inspirational and motivational – it's just that they never really worked for me. I must also clarify that I really enjoyed working with some people but others, well – we just didn't 'click', and occasionally there was one or two I could have quite happily 'clocked' (but, of course, never did).

Defining how you really feel about teamwork

I decided to work out why I found teamwork tricky, because there was one thing I knew for sure: I couldn't achieve what I wanted to achieve, in my career or in my life, on my own. If you also struggle with 'getting on the train' and playing nice with everyone in your team, think back to your childhood (focusing on around age eight to fifteen should do it) and ask yourself the following five questions while considering all of the different types of teams or groups you were part of – including sport, at school, after school, and family and friends. Once you're focused on your childhood self, think about the following:

1. Did you hide or stand up when teams were being formed? Why?
2. What was your favourite team experience and why?
3. What was your least favourite team experience and why?
4. Who was your favourite coach, teacher or leader and why?
5. Who was your least favourite coach, teacher or leader and why?

After I had a think about the preceding five questions, a picture of me as a kid, and so of me as an adult, started to emerge:

1. I'm not very competitive – I don't enjoy beating other people.
2. I am de-motivated by yelling, finger pointing and bad language.
3. I want everyone on a team to feel valued and respected.
4. I am most productive and most inspired if the aim of the team is to help others.
5. I like teams that are solution-focused – negativity and complaining does my head in.

How we felt about and responded to being in a team in our formative years can have an impact on how we feel about teamwork in the workplace. All of the insights outlined in the preceding list are still true for me today, but now I am less annoyed by co-worker differences. Why? Because I know how to explain my needs and how to find out what my team members need. I understand and am working on improving my emotional intelligence, I consider the four behavioural styles and I choose to keep learning about people.

If you want to thrive and not just survive in your team, I urge you to reflect and then take the next step. Identify who you need to recruit to your team – both your workplace team and your after-hours team.

> **To become and remain a customer service professional, you are going to need help both in and out of work.**

Your workplace team

Having people in your workplace that you can go to for help and support, as well as having people come to you for help and support is going to give you not only confidence but also a sense of purpose.

You may be allocated to a team or, in a large workplace, you may have opportunities for you to participate in different teams.

Here are a few examples of possible reasons for forming a team:

- audit and compliance
- events
- management/leadership
- recruitment
- special project.

The following sections take you through some steps to being a valued workplace team member, whatever the reason for the team being established.

Be friendly

Devote a portion of your day toward relationship building, even if it's just for ten minutes, perhaps broken up into two- or five-minute segments. For example, say hello to and smile at those you see at the beginning of your day or shift, ask a colleague for advice or offer to get them a coffee or a drink. If you're not used to doing this, go on, make the effort. If this is not something you usually do, it may feel strange at first and maybe your co-workers will be surprised or suspect you are angling for something from them, but as long as you are genuine and consistent, you have nothing to lose. These little interactions help build the foundation of good workplace relationships, especially if they're face to face.

Appreciate others

Show your appreciation whenever someone helps you. Everyone, from your boss to the office cleaner, wants to feel that their work is appreciated. So, genuinely compliment the people around you when they do something well.

Set boundaries

All of us like to have friends at work but, occasionally, a friendship can start to affect our jobs, especially when a friend or colleague begins to monopolise our time. If this happens, it's important that you're assertive about your boundaries, and that you know how much time you can devote during the work day for social interactions.

Avoid gossiping

Office politics and 'gossip' are major relationship killers at work. If you're experiencing conflict with someone at work, talk to them directly about the problem. Gossiping about the situation with other colleagues not only spreads the negative feelings but can also cause mistrust and animosity, and have a negative effect on the rest of your team.

Accept this

Occasionally, you'll have to work with someone you may not like or that you find difficult to relate to. For the sake of your career and everyone else in your team, it's essential you maintain professional relationships with everyone on your team. Whenever you are in this situation, instead of putting energy into focusing on what you don't like or understand about a co-worker, focus on finding things that you have in common.

Take the time to talk to them, and be open to learning about what makes them different to you. Remember – not all workplace relationships will be great; but you can make sure that they are at least workable.

Your after-hours team

Customer service professionals also have a team of people outside of work to help them not only achieve success in their chosen career but also reach that all important and much talked about state – work/life balance. Here are some people you should consider having on your after-hours team:

- *Mentors:* people you can ask questions of who will give you honest and useful support and guidance in your career.
- *Social connections:* stay in touch with friends and family who can help you to have fun, switch off and relax.
- *Health and fitness professionals:* include here mind and body specialists, such as allied health professionals, counsellors, physios, personal trainers, therapists, dieticians, chiropractors and GPs.
- *Personal development providers:* the more you know, the more you grow. Various adult education providers and volunteer programs are available that can give you new skills and provide you with the chance to help others grow as well.

Always be mindful when searching for support outside of your organisation that you are abiding by the privacy rules and regulations of your business.

Also remember the importance of 'me time' – time just for you doing exactly what makes you happy. This could be spending time with pets, going to the movies, writing, sleeping, driving, working on your art or listening to music.

Teamwork action

Create your own list of people you need to recruit to your workplace and after-hours teams. You may be surprised at how many people will be happy to help you.

U

IS FOR UNDERSTANDING EMPLOYER EXPECTATIONS

People will go where they can grow.

SETH GODIN

The 2012 edition of Graduate Careers Australia's employer directory *Graduate Opportunities* highlighted research from James Cook University that showed the most desired skills that employers from various industries are seeking in their employees are communication and interpersonal skills – over and above any industry-specific technical skills.

Employers today are assessing new recruits' communication and interpersonal skills, and providing training to refresh and improve those skills of their existing staff, for many reasons. Perhaps most importantly, customers willingly buy from and want to do business with people who are easy to interact with.

When an organisation gets these skills right, the acquisition of new customers automatically becomes much easier – and many other things become easier too. For example:

- Excellent service improves staff morale and motivation.
- When customers are happy, staff are happier too – and more productive.
- Reduced customer complaints naturally reduces the stress of the employees.
- Retaining customers enables the whole organisation to focus more on proactive opportunities (such as growth, innovation and development).
- Having a culture of delighting and retaining customers fuels positive publicity and a good reputation in the media and, increasingly, on the web in blogs and forums.
- Organisations with a positive workplace culture attract a higher calibre of job seekers.

Along with expecting good communication and interpersonal skills, organisations will have other expectations of their employees too. The following sections take you through some of these expectations.

The organisational structure

Depending on the size of the business you work for, many people could be holding various roles required for the business to achieve its goals. You may find that one person holds more than one role, and you may also find that more than one person holds the same role.

Some typical roles in business today include the following:

- administration/accounts/reception
- CEO/business owner/manager
- finance officer/accountant
- human resources/learning and development/training
- IT/programmer/technician
- labourer/apprentice/maintenance
- sales/marketing/media/PR/business development
- shop assistant/front desk/service staff
- supervisor/team leader/department manager
- waiter/waitress/chef/concierge.

Your organisation may also have a range of documents that will give you valuable information about the history and the goals of the business. Smaller businesses may not have all of these documents so you may have to speak with your direct manager to gain the information.

Here are the kinds of documents you could look out for:

- annual reports
- customer service charter
- meeting minutes
- organisational chart
- policies and procedures
- strategic plans
- vision and mission statements.

Accessing and reading through these kinds of documents, or talking to your direct manager about the kind of 'big picture' information they contain, will give you a better understanding of the organisation's overall aims and business approach. In turn, this will give you more of an idea of how your role fits in with this approach and the expectations that come with the role.

How and why business decisions are made

Businesses large and small use various procedures and processes to make decisions. Many things often need to be considered before making any decision, and part of the process will be to assess the impact those decisions may have on stakeholders.

Stakeholders in the organisation and in the decision can include any of the following:

- community
- customers
- environment
- governing bodies
- industry regulators
- investors
- shareholders
- staff
- suppliers.

Businesses today lean towards a more open and consultative approach with their employees, but it's simply not always possible and practical to run everything by everyone in the business. Part of being a customer service professional is being comfortable with not always knowing why and how business decisions are made. Customer service professionals understand that, sometimes, business decisions may have a negative impact on their role. This is exactly when a customer service professionals shines

– they consider the impact as a whole and not just how it affects them solely. Ultimately, this is what your employer expects from you.

Having held management and decision-making positions in the past and now as a business owner, I can confirm that it is much less stressful to focus solely on providing excellent customer service than to also have to make decisions that impact a range of stakeholders.

Feedback from the decision-makers

I regularly meet with employers and business owners to help them recruit and train customer service staff. This gives me great insights into many different types of businesses and the problems that they face when trying to build a team of customer service professionals. It also gives me a very clear idea on what these employers expect from their employees.

The following list summarises some of the comments I've received from employers from various industries when I asked them this one question: When you seek to hire employees who have to interact with your external customers, what do you look for?

Here is what those employers told me:

- 'Someone who is friendly and positive, and with a can-do attitude.' (Department store)
- 'A genuine desire to help people have a great experience.' (Hospitality)
- 'Great communicators who put the needs of the customer first.' (Accounting practice)
- 'An ability to change their behaviour to suit every customer.' (Property development)

- 'Excellent presentation and confidence when dealing with upset customers.' (School administration)
- 'The ability to multi-task and remain calm in the eyes of the customer.' (Water industry)
- 'Proactive staff who identify ways for us to improve our service.' (Truck sales)
- 'Staff with a positive attitude.' (Plumbing)
- 'Staff who work well together.' (Hairdressers)
- 'Proactive staff who are willing to go the extra mile for our customers.' (Book shop).

None of the employers said they wanted people with excellent technical (hard) skills. Employers can train people how to do the technical components of a job or they can assess those skills by asking for qualifications. But what they ache for is to find staff with high-level people (soft) skills. Soft skills increase the chances that the employees will get along with each other, and are the skills that have customers coming back and bringing all their friends and family with them.

> **Employees with excellent soft skills help to grow businesses.**

Understanding employer expectations action

If you have questions about what's expected of you in your role or don't fully understand the big picture of your business, be proactive and arrange to speak to your manager or relevant workplace contacts. Use these two steps to help you:

1. *Plan:* prepare suitable questions before you meet with the relevant individual/s. You may have your own specific questions but, if not, try these:

    - What three things are most important in my role of providing customer service?
    - What should I be prepared for when dealing with our customers?
    - What other areas of the business would it be good for me to learn about?
    - Where can I find relevant policies and procedures?

2. *Approach with respect:* Approach the relevant person or people and ask for a convenient time to catch up. This shows you are respectful of other people's time and that you have a genuine interest in representing the business in the best way possible. Confirm your intent is to learn so you can increase your confidence as a customer service provider.

Although this action is more suited to customer service providers who have just commenced in a role, consider using it even if you have been in the role for more than six months. It's never too late to be great. This one action alone will exceed your employer's expectation of you. Any employer who has customer service staff who take charge of their own learning is an employer who is jumping up and down in delight – they just might do it when you're not looking.

V

IS FOR VENTING

*A diamond is a chunk of coal that
did well under pressure.*

HENRY KISSINGER

When it comes to venting about your work (and perhaps your employer), you may have a different view to those around you. Have a think about the following:

- Do you like to vent to close friends or family about things that are causing you stress?
- Do you think that venting is a sign of weakness?
- Do you think that venting is a waste of time?
- Do you think that venting is a valuable way for you to help yourself?

In the 'E is for Emotional Intelligence' chapter, I shared with you the value of this kind of intelligence. And part of being emotionally intelligent is recognising when you need to step back and recharge your customer service batteries, gain perspective on why you are doing what you are doing and, in some cases, just stop thinking about work altogether.

What can happen when you don't vent

Before I share my story with you, please keep in mind that your response to workplace stress may be very different to mine. I want to share my story because many people have told me it has not only helped them to identify their own stress triggers, but also reminded them they need to be self-aware regarding their own stress levels.

After more than 15 years of working in the bank, one day I arrived at work, walked in the front door and just couldn't stay there. I had this overwhelming feeling of having to leave. I walked to my desk, grabbed my coffee cup and a couple of other things, and then walked into my boss's office, sat down and said, 'I'm done.'

My boss looked at me with genuine surprise and said, 'What do you mean?' I remember that tears were running down my face but I wasn't actually crying. I said, 'I'm sorry; I just can't be here anymore.' He was very concerned, and suggested I have a day or two off.

I did and I also rang the Employee Assistance Program (EAP) that the bank provided. The EAP service put me in touch with a local counsellor, who advised I needed to take some leave and attend some counselling sessions.

After three weeks away from the workplace and three one-hour sessions with the counsellor, I started to make sense of what had happened. Many terms were used to describe my situation – including stress, burnout, anxiety and depression – but I called it 'people fatigue' and the 'plight of a perfectionist'. Indeed, my counsellor agreed that those titles also were suited to my situation.

With the help of my counsellor, I learned that the reasons for my 'walk out' were quite extensive, and that they had been slowly but surely building up over time. Here are a few of the things I identified as the causes that led to me feeling overwhelmed and in need of a break:

- being unaware how a competitive environment was de-motivating me and causing me anxiety
- being naturally submissive to the needs of others – putting myself second
- not understanding my personality type and how different it was from many of my co-workers
- feeling stuck – I believed I had no other career choices
- spending most of my day listening to and having to handle complaints and negativity – from staff and customers
- doing more than was needed in the role – aiming for perfection in everything I did
- ignoring my gut instincts regarding stress – soldiering on
- not getting independent perspectives and support – only venting my concerns to co-workers.

Before this situation, I was very sceptical about the counselling process. Perhaps like many others in similar situations, I was of the mind that there was no way a stranger (that is, the counsellor) would be able to understand my work situation, let alone provide help, simply by talking. How could they understand me if I couldn't? I was sure any process would take too long and I would have to share too much before they could help me. I also thought, *I'm an adult – this is something I should be able to handle myself.*

The EAP counselling, however, was highly beneficial for me. Indeed, the process changed my mind about the value of venting to a professional. I was amazed at how much clarity I gained from just three one-hour sessions and also from being out of the workplace. Time out helped me to put things into perspective, and I felt strong again and confident. With some practical and achievable coping strategies, I was able to return to work – although not for long.

I was clear that I needed a new career path and, when the opportunity came, I made the decision to leave the bank. I left at the age of 32, with no job in sight, a mortgage and Year 10 qualifications. But rather than feeling scared, I had never felt more confident and excited. I had what I needed – I had a plan.

With the help of my counsellor I developed a plan that included me engaging a career coach, and this coach helped me apply for and gain a job in a disability employment service. This was a role that would benefit from my natural talents of helping, caring and teaching. I finished my diploma of business and also commenced a diploma in counselling. I didn't want to be a counsellor but I wanted to understand the history, the theories and the strategies that people use today to process negative or stressful thoughts and feelings. I wanted to understand venting in the professional sense.

How workplaces can help you become mentally healthy

According to the Australian Human Rights Commission, mental illness is more prevalent in Australia than many people realise, with around 45 per cent of Australians aged between 16 and 85 experiencing a mental illness at some point in their life. And when it comes to mental health and your working environment, the commission argues that 'an "unhealthy" work environment or a workplace incident can cause considerable stress and exacerbate, or contribute to, the development of mental illness'.

The commission highlights that employers have legal obligations in relation to the management of mental illness in the workplace, such as ensuring health and safety, avoiding discrimination, ensuring privacy and avoiding adverse actions for any employee with mental illness.

In turn, all workers (including those with mental illness) also have obligations, including taking reasonable care for their own health and safety and taking care that their acts and omissions do not adversely affect the health or safety of others. Employees should also cooperate with any reasonable instructions to ensure workplace health and safety. (To read more information from the Australian Human Rights Commission on mental illness at work, go to www.humanrights.gov.au and search 'mental health in the workplace'.)

So employers and employees have obligations with regard to mental health, and your employer is there to help. Further, customer service professionals know that for them to provide a consistently superior level of service, their mental health is of vital importance. Within this, venting is a strategy to help keep you mentally healthy.

Start to think of venting as a positive strategy to improve your mental health. Your friends, family and co-workers will likely want to help you through tough times, and they are a valuable source of support. If you find yourself not being able to move on from negative thoughts or feelings about any area of your life, however, consider professional venting.

So how do I vent now? I have a mentor, I have an accountability group and I have business associates who I meet with regularly and we allow each other to vent. I know what can cause me stress and anxiety and I know that mental health symptoms and solutions can be different for everyone.

I know that having and accessing support for my mental health is not weak.

> There is no greater sign of strength than asking for someone else to lift you up.

Venting action

Stop. Reflect. Turn off all the noise. Sit with yourself and think about your own mental health. The act of sitting still and thinking about how we feel can be confronting for some but give it a go. For you to be bright, friendly and helpful in your role as a customer service provider, the first person you have to look after is you.

Use these steps as a guide:

1. Write down the event/s that cause or caused you stress at work.
2. Identify if there is a theme – is it one person, similar situations or locations that cause the stress?
3. Share your concerns with a trusted friend or co-worker.
4. Tell that person you want them to give you some practical solutions.
5. If you still find yourself in need of input or support, consider a professional vent buddy.

W

IS FOR WORST-CASE SCENARIOS

Anxiety is the price we pay
for being unprepared.

ANONYMOUS

Perhaps you have skipped everything else in this book and landed straight at this chapter. Welcome, this is a safe place for you to land. I am going to share with you my own experiences of surviving some pretty horrible situations.

Firstly, however, being clear on what I mean by the term 'worst-case scenario' is important. For me, a worst-case scenario has always been any interaction with a customer that makes my hands start to shake and the desire to escape becomes overwhelming. In other words, I can tell by the way my body reacts to situations as to whether or not I feel safe.

Some examples of my own worst-case scenarios include:

- being physically pushed by a customer who was demanding to enter the bank after-hours
- witnessing two customers fist-fighting in front of me, resulting in lots of blood, and the need for an ambulance and the police
- being harassed after-hours via telephone hang ups and heavy breathing
- having an empty beer bottle thrown at me from across the street by two unhappy customers while I was walking back from lunch (luckily it missed); the incident included aggressive verbal abuse
- having a customer threaten to jump the counter and attack one of my staff
- being verbally abused and threatened over the phone – the threats were so specific the police were called and security guards employed
- having a customer phoning me and advising he was going to blow up the workplace – and the person was an ex–Navy SEAL so the threat was taken *very* seriously.

My very first worst-case scenario was being yelled at by a customer, in full view of other customers. It was horrible. The customer, who was taller than me, approached me with no warning, stood very close to me, pointed his finger in my face and, at the top of his voice, said I was useless at my job and demanded to see the manager.

I was fifteen, had no training as to what I should do in that situation, and was shocked but also anxious about what the customer might do next. I quickly got the manager and went and hid out of sight. I don't rate this type of interaction as a worst-case scenario anymore – I lived through it and learned that this type of bad customer behaviour can happen. Although it felt personal, it wasn't. It was an emotional customer who was unable to control his temper. He apologised to my manager … later.

You will rarely get a warning that a worst-case scenario is going to happen and, other than the event itself, it's the lack of warning that really does make it a worst-case scenario. In all of the cases in the preceding list, I had no warning beforehand and every time I had the same physical response: heart beating faster, hands shaking and a general feeling of fear and that I wanted to remove myself from the situation immediately. Those responses are human and are based on our built-in safety program – our fight or flight response. This is your body's natural response to a perceived threat or danger, and includes the release of hormones like adrenaline and cortisol, which speed up the heart and divert blood flow away from functions like digestion and to major muscle groups. All this primes the body for a burst of energy and strength – to either take on the perceived threat or run far away from it. According to Young Diggers:

> *Originally named for its ability to enable us to physically fight or run away when faced with danger, it's now activated in situations where neither response is appropriate, like in traffic or during a stressful day at work. When the perceived threat is gone, systems are designed to return to normal function via the relaxation response, but in our times of chronic stress, this often doesn't happen enough, causing damage to the body.*

For more information on the fight or flight response, see www.youngdiggers.com.au/fight-or-flight.

If you feel violated, threatened or abused in the workplace, you must not ignore this feeling.

Why some customers behave aggressively

Customers often avoid complaining until they deem it absolutely necessary or believe they have enough 'ammunition' to strengthen their case. By that time they may have become anxious, upset or angry, and so may have lost the ability to communicate effectively.

Some people believe that raising their voice, pointing their fingers and even having an audience will get a complaint resolved in their favour. Others like to ambush us, demanding answers and giving us no time to collect our thoughts.

All of these, and more, are examples of difficult behaviours used by customers. Many factors can contribute to why people use such behaviours, including:

- examples from role models – such as family, teachers, leaders and coaches
- fear and anxiety – such as fear of looking stupid, feeling left out, fear of losing
- financial and time concerns
- previously rewarded behaviour – the behaviour has worked before so will likely work again
- mental or physical health issues
- substance abuse
- level of emotional intelligence (see 'E is for Emotional Intelligence' for more).

Part of being a customer service professional is making yourself available to strangers or people who you may not normally chose to associate with. In my career, these interactions have been not only challenging but also at times distressing, and I've needed time away from work to help me recover.

Handling the aftershock

Angry, frustrated or confused people can break our concentration, raise our stress levels and make it difficult to do our jobs safely and efficiently. I usually find that after any worst-case scenario, I feel quite drained and often want to retreat and lie down. I call this feeling 'aftershock'. Your aftershock may have a different effect on you but no matter what, it is important that you take a moment to check in with yourself and to use your emotional intelligence to identify and then manage your feelings.

To understand how the stress of worst-case scenarios can affect you over the long term, think of your aftershock like a glass of water. How heavy do you think a glass of water is? No matter the size of the glass or how full it is, its weight will be affected by how long you hold the glass. If you only hold it for a few moments, the glass might feel light; the longer you hold it, however, the heavier it feels. This is like aftershock – the longer you hold onto negative thoughts or feelings, the more taxing or heavier they can become.

To help you calm after a worst-case scenario, Young Diggers recommend the three-part breath process, which includes finding a quiet place to sit or lie down, and focusing on deep, calm breathing. For a full rundown and further tips, go to www.youngdiggers.com.au/fight-or-flight and click the 'Taming the fight or flight response' link.

Remember – the idea that we all have to be 'tough' and handle everything that happens to us both quickly and professionally when we are at work is unnecessary and ultimately bad for yourself, your co-workers and the business. Worst-case scenarios are not everyday occurrences and should not be treated as such.

Resist the urge to 'soldier on' and be prepared that your aftershock may be delayed.

The good news about worst-case scenarios

As well as being aware of the need to deal appropriately with the after-shock of any worst-case scenarios, the following sections may also help.

Worst-case scenarios are rare

I've been working in customer service roles for over 32 years and my experience of eight worst-case scenarios (which I outlined at the start of this chapter) means, on average, I have had one experience every four years. I can't guarantee that more won't occur in my future but I know for sure that help is available and this alone allows me to relax and feel confident that when the next one happens, I'll be okay.

Help is available

Professional help is available and you should avail yourself of this, even if you use it simply to have someone to hear you talk through what happened. Access the support that your employer provides or seek ideas from your GP. I have heard of bank employees taking on long-term professional support to manage their response to a hold-up, for example. The support was not only required by the people directly involved in the hold-up, either, but also by those who were in the branch at the time – including customers and also staff who were not present. Those directly involved in the event need the understanding and support from their colleagues, so those colleagues also need to be supported.

Worst-case scenarios action

If you only do some of the actions from this book, please do this: identify your potential worst-case scenario and speak to your employer to confirm what you are to do if that event happens.

Extra things you might want to suggest to your employer include:

- inviting the local police or a security service to attend a team meeting to share strategies that help to create a safe environment
- asking your team to identify their concerns and discussing these as a team to find solutions
- contacting your industry or governing body for best safety practices
- practising all evacuation and drills, regularly
- having emergency numbers by the phone
- setting up customer meeting rooms so staff members sit closest to the door – offering them a quick escape if the customer becomes agitated
- considering personal alarms for staff members who find themselves in a threatening situation but are away from co-worker support.

X

IS FOR X FACTOR

An 'X factor' is a variable in a given situation that could have the most significant impact on the outcome.

GOOGLE DEFINITIONS

Do you know what your 'X factor' is as a customer service provider? You are unique and your uniqueness is valuable as a customer service provider – so welcome to the chapter that can only be written by you. Some of you might find this chapter confronting. Others may find it a little embarrassing to complete the activity I am about to share with you. If this is the case, I urge you to step outside of your comfort zone and be willing to find your X factor.

Finding your X factor

I first completed an exercise similar to the one I am about to share when I was in between jobs – after the bank and before disability employment. At the time, I had what I thought were very limited job prospects, and was sure that the skills I had would only be suited to another bank. This limited thinking caused me anxiety, because the last thing I wanted to do was work in another bank. When I engaged a career coach, however, she helped alter my perception of my workplace skills, confirming that my soft skills were transferrable and every businesses wanted employees with excellent soft skills.

She also gave me this activity. I was to select five people I knew well, and ask them to answer this one question: 'What do you think are my natural talents?'

This activity made me feel uncomfortable, because I was sure asking friends or family to answer this question would make them think I was seeking compliments. And what if they couldn't think of anything? My coach told me to relax and to remember that this activity wasn't about asking for compliments; it was about finding out what other people identify as your strengths. A person who knows and likes you will have no trouble coming up with your attributes. Further, what you think you are good at may or may not be what others identify. You might also find out that you have strengths you didn't even know about.

So, I plucked up the courage and stepped outside of my comfort zone and selected my five people. I told them that I had to do this to help me in my search for a new job. If you're not sure how to gain this information without coming off as self-seeking or desperate for compliments, try something like this: 'I'm reading this great book so I can become a customer service professional and the author suggests I would benefit from learning how people perceive me. I only need you to answer one question and you can write down or tell me your answer. I selected you because you know me well and I need the perspective of someone I trust and respect.'

This activity gives you great insight into how your customers might perceive you. Even if you spend your day assessing everything you do and how you do it, you won't know for sure how others perceive you. We are often harder on ourselves than we need to be so take a deep breath and accept the challenge of finding out how other people view you and your natural talents. This is your X factor.

> Customer service professionals could win an Olympic gold if customer service was an event. They use all their resources, combined with their X factor, to provide a level of service that not only delights but also surprises the customers.

X factor action

1. Ask yourself what you think are your natural talents before you ask anyone else.

2. Select five people to interview and ask them the question: 'What do you think are my natural talents?' Choose five people who come from different areas of your life and will give you honest and useful answers. Use this list to help you identify your five people:

   - best friend
   - coach
   - co-worker or workplace colleague
   - direct supervisor or manager
   - family member
   - mentor
   - partner
   - social friend
   - teacher
   - trainer
   - work friend

3. Collate their responses and write them down.

4. When you get your answers, ask yourself these questions and note down your thoughts:

- Where there any answers that surprised you? Why or why not?
- Do you already use those skills when interacting with your internal customers?
- Do you already use those skills when interacting with external customers?
- What skills were not identified that you thought you were showing to others?
- What skills were identified by more than one person?
- What skills would you like to be known for that weren't identified?
- How could you improve those skills?

Y

IS FOR YOUR FUTURE

While some industries have automated aspects of their service needs – allowing passengers to check themselves in for a flight, for example – good staff are far and away the most crucial element of good service.

SERVICE 2020: MEGATRENDS FOR THE DECADE AHEAD
(AVAILABLE VIA WWW.BDO.CO.UK)

The internet has given us the ability to research, compare and purchase products and services online, with little or no contact with a customer service person. We can have our transactions processed quickly, at any time of the day and from the comfort of our own home. So what could this mean for your future as a provider of customer service? Is the end near? Will there be less need for customer service professionals?

I have done the research for you and here's what I found: according to the *Service 2020* report, 'the vast majority (82 per cent) of firms polled believe that no matter what technological innovations are in the pipeline, customers will always expect some form of personal interaction in customer service'.

What customers will want in the future

The *Service 2020* findings show that more than ever, the customer is going to drive how businesses operate in the future. The report also shows that businesses recognise that Gen Y and beyond are seeking instant responses to their queries and instant access to their desired products, so businesses will certainly have to look at developing a 24/7 platform, if they don't already have one in place, so their customers don't shop elsewhere. But consider this:

- Would you prefer your restaurant meal be self-serve?
- Would you be happy to go to a hospital with no human carers?
- Would you feel comfortable leaving your child in a day care centre with no people?
- Do you always want to limit your purchasing decision to just two of your five senses – sight and sound?

Change is guaranteed. Roles will change, technology will advance and what we consider effective and efficient may be radically different in the next decade – or even in the next 12 months. No matter what changes in business, however, people will still want to do business with people. What this means for the future is that the demand for employees who interact directly with customers to have the skills of a customer service professional will increase – these skills will be required to keep customers coming back.

> Customer service professionals accept that change is constant in today's workforce but they can rest easy knowing that their skills will always be in high demand.

Insight into three high-growth industries

According to the Federal Department of Employment:

> *Employment is projected to increase in 16 of the 19 broad industries over the five years to November 2020. Health Care and Social Assistance is projected to make the largest contribution to employment growth (increasing by 250,200), followed by Professional, Scientific and Technical Services (151,200), Education and Training (121,700) and Retail Trade (106,000). Together, these four industries are projected to provide more than half of total employment growth over the five years to November 2020.*

These figures highlight the high-growth areas for Australian industries, and so the areas of growing employment opportunities (see www.employment.gov.au to find out more). Within these four broad industries, I've identified three specific high-growth industries – covered in the following sections.

Aged care

We are living in healthy times. Never before have we lived for so long and had so many people to look after. This means, of course, that our aged-care services are in high demand – and that demand is only going to get higher, so this is definitely one area where customer service professionals will be in demand. Indeed, as HealthTimes highlights:

> Australia currently has about 2,800 residential aged care facilities providing care to more than 160,000 elderly people. Over the next ten years, the number of residents is projected to reach more than 250,000 and the highest area of growth will be among residents aged 95 or over.

You can go to www.healthtimes.com.au to find out more about the current and projected state of Australian aged care.

Aged-care facilitates require a range of positions filled that all require a high level of customer service skills – for example:

- administrators
- bus drivers
- cleaners
- gardeners
- health-care providers
- liaison officers
- maintenance people – plumbers, builders, carpenters
- managers
- receptionists
- recreational/activity staff
- security.

Entrepreneurialism

It's being hailed as a revolution: individuals around the world are moving out of the corporate world and starting their own businesses. You may want to start your own business one day and, if so, your people (soft) skills are going to be vital. You're going to need to get people to work for you and, of course, buy your products and services. The best entrepreneurs outsource the work they can't do or are less skilled in so they are free to do the work they love. Outsourcing means communicating with people, and you are also going to need to be able to educate and motivate these people to provide you with their best work.

Even before you get to starting your own business, the growth of entrepreneurialism and subsequent outsourcing of certain tasks, can also provide valuable employment. I am part of a large group of entrepreneurs and we are always seeking people such as the following to help grow our business:

- bookkeepers/accountants
- brand experts
- business coaches
- image consultants
- lawyers
- marketers
- personal assistants/virtual assistants
- photographers
- publishers/editors
- social media specialists
- videographers
- website designers.

Entrepreneurs also seek help with their personal lives from the following service providers:

- child carers
- cleaners

- cooks
- counsellors
- personal shoppers
- personal trainers.

IT *roles*

The IT industry is already crying out for staff who have great people skills. The industry has a plentiful supply of staff with fantastic technical (hard) skills but often these staff members lack the people (soft) skills to interact with each other and their customers. Not many businesses keep their IT staff away from their customers, and the amount of frustration and confusion that happens between the IT employees, the non-IT employees and the customers is, well, a reason for quite a large portion of my business.

If this industry interests you, get ahead of the competition by investing in some people skills training.

Landing the job of your dreams

Landing the job of your dreams may seem just around the corner, or it may seem impossible. In this section, I provide some tips to help make it a reality.

Before I get to these more specific tips, first remember to always focus on building and highlighting your emotional intelligence. As I've mentioned in previous chapters, businesses today not only recognise that emotional intelligence (EQ) is a key predictor of employee job satisfaction and success, but also actively assess the EQ level of job candidates and determine how they will fit into their workplace and meet the needs of their customers.

Now to get into the detail of finding and securing your dream job. You can search for jobs via the internet or newspapers but also remember that often businesses will advertise their vacancies on their websites. Once you find a job you're interested in, you may find that some businesses will want you to provide just your resume, others may want a cover letter and, for more senior or government roles, you may also have to provide answers to key selection criteria (KSC). The KSC is simply a set of questions that ask you to provide a written response to each question to further detail your skills and experiences.

If you haven't applied for a job for a while or are unsure of the right style of resume and other requirements, you may wish to use a recruitment service to help with the process. Again, you can find your local recruitment services via the internet or newspapers and using these services is a great way to make sure you are using the most up-to-date resume templates and completing the most effective job seeking activities. Private providers also can help with creating your resume and completing job applications, although this usually comes at a cost.

Your ability to prove you have the soft skills and the passion to provide consistently superior customer service has to come across early when you are seeking employment. Use the following ten steps to help land your dream job by showing you are a customer service professional online, on paper and face to face:

1. *Build a LinkedIn profile*: LinkedIn is kind of like Facebook but for business profiles, and employers often seek to find employees via their LinkedIn profiles. Like Facebook, it's free to use and you can create your own profile but remember – unlike Facebook this platform is not for personal posts. It's a business platform

so present yourself professionally. If you're unsure about what to put on your profile, look at other profiles to get some great ideas.

2. *Polish your resume:* Resumes are still valued so keep yours up to date and include that you understand the value of soft skills in customer service roles.

3. *Nurture your referees:* Keep your referees current and aware that you are applying for jobs.

4. *Write a strong cover letter:* Use a cover letter for all job applications, but never use the same cover letter for different jobs. Doing so is certainly quicker but remember: employers want customer service professionals so this is a chance to prove you are willing to go over and above what is expected. Do some research on what the business does and weave this knowledge into the cover letter, along with how you will work to build strong workplace relationships – with both the business's internal and external customers.

5. *Arrive early:* Always be early for a job interview (ten to fifteen minutes is more than enough).

6. *Work on your presentation carefully:* Re-read (or read) the 'P is for Presentation' chapter for tips.

7. *Acknowledge any nerves:* If you fear you will be nervous and that you won't be able to control nervous tendencies (such as a shaking voice, red face or sweaty hands) it's okay to confirm to the interviewer/s that you are a bit nervous because you are very excited about this opportunity. Deep breathing can help settle your nerves.

8. *Be considered:* Take your time answering questions and ask for questions to be repeated if you're not sure what the interviewer is seeking. Interviewers get nervous too.

9. *Ask questions:* Have at least one question ready to ask the interviewer/s. The question you ask should be relevant to the business or the role you are applying for. Review the business's website and form questions to suit – for example, 'Can you tell me more about how this business started?', 'What do you see as the main aim of this role?' or 'What skills do you value in this role?'

10. *Finish well:* Thank the interviewer/s for their time and confirm you look forward to hearing from them. How you leave them feeling will remain in their minds, so leave them feeling that you are professional.

Your future action

Employers today use behavioural questions to uncover a candidate's natural behavioural style and to also get a sense of their soft skills. Customer service professionals arrive at interviews prepared to answer these behavioural questions.

Take your time when answering interview questions and remember that asking for a question to be repeated if you are unsure is better than rushing in, speaking too quickly and coming off as unable to control your emotions. Also remember that body language and tone of voice carry the information of how you feel and what your attitude is.

To prepare for your interview, think about your answers to these potential questions:

1. Explain a time when you had to deal with an angry customer. What happened and what did you do?
2. A customer asks you questions you don't know the answer to. What do you do?
3. A co-worker has told a customer the wrong information. What do you do?
4. You are on the phone when a customer approaches you. What do you do?
5. You need to speak to a co-worker who is with a customer. The matter is urgent. What do you do?

Z

IS FOR ZEN

The quieter you become,
the more you can hear.

RAM DASS

As we get into the art of Zen, ask yourself:

- How do you switch off after a busy day?
- Do you have a specific activity that helps you to relax?
- Do you find it hard to sleep after a day or a week spent dealing with difficult people or in peak periods?

According to www.urbandictionary.com:

One way to think of Zen is this: a total state of focus that incorporates a total togetherness of body and mind. Zen is a way of being. It also is a state of mind. Zen involves dropping illusion and seeing things without distortion created by your own thoughts.

As you can imagine, I have engaged with hundreds of customer service professionals and, during our chats, I've gained great insight into what keeps them awake at night – and also how they control their mind chatter and reach a state of Zen. I use 'mind chatter' to describe that discussion going on in your head that could be about many things – including unsatisfactory outcomes of discussions, outstanding tasks, pending difficult decisions, financial concerns, health issues, future deadlines, what ifs and how comes … you get the picture.

When our minds take over with negative or nagging thoughts, they can be hard to turn off and, depending on the level of anxiety the chatter creates, some people find it hard to sleep.

Finding your Zen

During the research for this book, I met some wonderful practitioners who are dedicated to helping people relax, unwind, focus on the positive and calm the mind chatter – or as they liked to suggest, be in the moment.

You may already have a preferred way of 'switching off' but if you're yet to find what works for you, I've included in this section a few examples of professional services that might be of assistance. Do some research to find out which one would suit you and give it a go.

Here are some options to get you started:

- emotional freedom techniques – for example, tapping specific areas on the body to release specific mental or physical issues
- facials
- massages

- personal trainers
- Pilates
- reiki
- yoga.

As most of the items on the preceding list require the help of another person, at least initially, sometimes it's good to find your own way of reaching a state of Zen. The following sections outline some examples of what customer service professionals do to relax after difficult interactions and to help them sleep soundly.

Practise mindfulness

Be present. Resist the urge to think about the past or the future. Sit comfortably and close your eyes. Starting with your feet, focus your attention on reducing any tension. Move up your body, giving attention to each area that is feeling tense or sore. Breathe deeply and slowly while doing this activity. If your mind wanders, that's okay. Give yourself permission to have the thought but then tell yourself you will address it later and bring yourself back to right now. Practising mindfulness for as little as ten minutes can greatly reduce feelings of stress or anxiety.

Pause

A great way to manage your mind chatter is to pause. The purpose of the pause is to shift attention from the emotional (limbic) to the analytical (cortex) part of your brain. By using your cortex, your brain can take as little as six seconds to slow down the flood of chemicals that are driving your emotions. Once the emotions have settled, you can analyse the issue rationally.

You can **cheat** your brain into calming down with the following:

- **c**omplete a puzzle
- **h**um or sing your favourite song
- **e**ngage in a conversation unrelated to the issue
- **a**dd up some sums or count the items on your desk
- **t**hink of six of your favourite TV characters.

Listen to music

Create two playlists – one to relax and one to uplift. If you need to wake up and gain more energy, go with the uplift list; if you feel stressed or a bit 'edgy' and you want to calm down, go with the relax playlist. Having the play lists pre-prepared makes it easier for you to access them – the stress of trying to find your favourite music can increase the stress you are already feeling or make you feel even more tired.

Seek feedback

Had a difficult interactional with a customer or a co-worker and not sure how you could have handled it better? Or perhaps you're feeling that you did your best but the other party was still unhappy?

Talk it through with a trusted co-worker in a private setting after you have had a chance to calm down or pause.

> A fresh perspective can help you 'see' the interaction more clearly. Be open to hearing constructive feedback.

Switch off

Make a conscious effort to leave work, switch off, and get ready for your after-work life. For example:

- When you put your car key in the ignition, choose to switch on the car and switch off work.
- When you reach your first red traffic light, take this as a sign to stop thinking about work when it turns green and start readying yourself for home (or wherever your after-work life is taking you).

If you don't drive home from work, think of other steps in your journey home to use in a similar way. Perhaps scanning your ticket or travel pass at the train station is your time to switch off work, or perhaps the first station the train stops at is the time to start readying yourself for your after-work life.

Be kind to yourself

Before you leave work, write down one thing you could have done better and three things you did well. Leave work feeling positive and know that you will be better at that one thing next time.

Laughter

A good belly laugh is a great way to relieve stress. Have your favourite jokes nearby or a picture you can look at that always makes you laugh. (Make sure pictures or jokes are not offensive to other workers.)

Balance

Aim for a balanced and healthy lifestyle that includes:

- a nutritious diet with plenty of fruit and vegetables

- regular exercise that gets your heart pumping
- adequate sleep most nights of the week.

De-brief wisely

Genuine friends offer positive support and advice, whereas uninterested colleagues may be negative, unhelpful and prone to gossip. De-briefing or venting can be a great way to lower your stress but always be mindful of when, where and who you choose to debrief with.

Make time for YOU

As much as your work and family life are important, it's just as important that you schedule some 'me time'. Taking just one hour, once a week to do something for yourself can do wonders for your wellbeing, your relationships and your career.

Keep learning

Stress or anxiety can be eased by seeking to learn more about the people, places or things that we don't fully understand. Thanks to the internet, you have access to unlimited sources of information but remember – just because it is on the internet does not automatically mean it is true or correct. Always check the source, and use multiple sources.

Access professional support

Whether your stress or anxiety is work or non-work related, if you prefer to seek outside support many options are available to you. Your general practitioner (GP) can provide you with options such as counsellors or psychologists or, if available, you can contact your workplace's Employee Assistance Program (EAP) or similar.

Other organisations are also there to help, such as:

- Beyond Blue (www.beyondblue.org.au)
- Lifeline (www.lifeline.org.au)
- Relationships Australia (www.relationshipsaustralia.org.au).

Have a pre-sleep plan

If your stress or anxiety is preventing you from getting a good night's sleep, sometimes a pre-sleep plan can help:

- consider a leisurely evening walk – speed is not necessary
- make lists so you won't go to bed with things on your mind
- turn off phones and devices
- avoid caffeine or other stimulants
- have a warm bath or shower
- relax your muscles by starting with your feet – refer to the 'Practise mindfulness' section for more.

If this plan (or counting sheep) doesn't work, I find another process very helpful if I can't sleep: for every letter of the alphabet, I mentally create specific lists, focusing on creating lists of things that are positive and make me smile. This activity helps to switch on your positive emotions brain and takes a bit of work so can help to tire your brain out.

Topic ideas include:

- favourite foods – apple, banana, cheesecake …
- destinations you would love to visit – Africa, Barbados, California …
- people you love and value
- places you've been and want to revisit
- favourite movies or books.

Get organised

If you're always running late, set your clock and watches fast and give yourself extra time. If your desk is a mess, file and throw away the clutter; just knowing where everything is saves you time and cuts stress. Make a to-do list and cross off items as you accomplish them. In peak periods or times of stress, the simple act of seeing what you have accomplished can give you a much needed positivity boost.

Zen action

Close your eyes and picture yourself relaxing. What are you doing? Where are you? What can you see, taste, touch, smell and hear?

Maybe it's a beach on a warm day with no-one else around and you have your favourite book and drink beside you and you can feel the sand between your toes. Perhaps you prefer to be walking in the bush and hearing the birds. Maybe relaxing for you is driving on the open road with your favourite songs playing.

The next time you find yourself needing to relax, close your eyes and take yourself to your 'happy place' and allow yourself to unwind. Our minds are amazing; we can take ourselves anywhere we want to – it just takes focus.

If your happy place is the beach on a warm day with no-one else around and you have your favourite book and drink beside you … look around, you might see me there (which defeats the purpose of being alone, so unless I wave you over, pick up your stuff and find another beach).

CONCLUSION

Too many times I meet people in workplaces who introduce themselves as, 'I'm *just* a receptionist' or 'I'm *just* a checkout operator/teller/administrator/waiter/waitress/call centre operator/retail assistant/personal assistant (the list goes on)'. The word 'just' tells me that they don't understand the value they have in the workplace.

Customer service professionals never consider themselves as *just* anything. They know they are a vital part of the business they work for and they know how to have customers and employers raving about them for all the right reasons. They know their value.

I wrote this book to give you the knowledge and the skills to take control of your career – because if you choose to become a customer service professional, your career opportunities will increase, your job and personal satisfaction will improve and you will experience less stress.

Whether you are a volunteer or a paid employee, your people skills are the skills that make the difference to your day and to the day of those you interact with. The world needs more customer service professionals.

My passion for helping people become customer service professionals has come from three events in my life.

The first was in March 1983 when my brother Timothy Francis Brennan was diagnosed with acute lymphatic leukaemia. In November 1983, Tim passed away. I was thirteen when Tim was diagnosed and fourteen when he died. He was twenty-three when he died. It was tough and I learned the hard way that life can be short.

The second event occurred between 1992 and 1995. During these years I experienced symptoms of multiple sclerosis. I adopted healthy lifestyle changes and to this day I monitor my health and am grateful that the disease has not progressed.

The third event occurred over the course of my working life, from age 15 to 32. By 32 I realised my generally bright, friendly and positive demeanour had been wearing away – even though I hadn't been aware it was happening along the way. I needed help, I got help and I changed my own future.

What have those three things got to do with writing this book? They taught me that life is a like a jigsaw puzzle:

- You don't know how long it will take.
- You need lots of different pieces.
- Some pieces will fit straight away but, no matter how hard you try, some pieces aren't meant to fit.
- All the pieces are required to make the big picture.
- It's easier and you can do more when you have help.

I have a genuine passion for helping people enjoy their workplace interactions and I have a genuine passion for living a life that helps others.

I wish I had this book earlier in my career. I wish I knew it was possible to identify jobs that would benefit my natural behavioural style. I wish I knew what support was available to help me in the tough times.

I want to save you this anxiety and show you how to have as much job satisfaction as possible. I want to help people communicate more confidently and interact more honestly. I want workplaces to become places we go to learn and not just to earn.

I have written this book to fulfil these aims and so I can reach as many people as possible. My business Lightbulb Training Solutions and this book is my way of making a positive difference in the lives of others. I'd love to hear your feedback or any stories you have from your customer service journey. You can get in touch with me via Facebook (www.facebook.com/lightbultrainingsolutions), my website (www.lightbulbtraining.com.au) or email (admin@lightbulbtraining.com.au).

REVIEW OF ALL CHAPTERS

Attitude – the one thing you have complete control over.
Choose wisely.

Behavioural Styles – knowing the four styles gives you great power.

Communication – it's more than what you say.

Detective – get to know your customers well and reap the rewards.

Emotional Intelligence – your EQ is more important than your IQ.

Fun – it's good for you and great for your workplace.

Generation Gaps – fill the gap with understanding.

Handling Complaints – LEAD your customers to a more positive emotional state.

Internal Motivation – you have to identify your WIIFM.

Juggling – you can do it with practise.

Knowledge – keep learning.

Listening – you learn nothing while you are talking.

Mystery Shoppers – staff performance is no longer a secret.

Non-negotiable – you've been warned.

Over and Above – fill up the bank of service excellence, but be careful: there is such a thing as too much.

Presentation – take care with your first and last impressions.

Quality and Quantity – know the difference and stay focused.

Reality Checks – take a breath and step back.

Selling – it's not hard when you know how.

Teamwork – you cannot do this alone.

Understanding Employer Expectations – know what they want and why.

Venting – take the lid off and cool down.

Worst-case Scenarios – identify and prepare for these, and reduce your anxiety.

X Factor – what's yours?

Your Future – it looks bright.

Zen – your place to relax.